WE ARE ONE

To Betty,

Lots of love to a very
dear friend,

Melanie xx

WE ARE ONE

Who are you?
What is your purpose
in this life?

Melanie Hallett

A record of this publication is available from the British Library.

ISBN 978-1-910027-07-3

Typesetting by Wordzworth Ltd
www.wordzworth.com

Cover design by Titanium Design Ltd
www.titaniumdesign.co.uk

Printed by Lightning Source UK
www.lightningsource.com

Cover image by Sylvie Gotti

Published by Local Legend
www.local-legend.co.uk

This book is dedicated to all those spirit people,
both in the body and beyond,
who have helped me to unfold spiritually thus far.

ABOUT THE AUTHOR

The Reverend Melanie Hallett grew up in what she calls "a spooky environment", attuned from a very young age to the spiritual worlds and to the heartbeat of nature. "Mediumship is normal to me," she says, "and not being that way is not." She began to train her abilities while still in her teens, was serving in Spiritualist churches at nineteen, and was already healing and teaching in her twenties. She is now acclaimed for her rare gifts of trance mediumship, demonstrating transfiguration and voice phenomena.

A minister of the Spiritualist religion and a member of The Healing Trust, Melanie now works internationally and has been featured many times in the press and on national and local television and radio.

Her personal path in life, however, has been far from easy and she has faced severe physical and emotional challenges. These have served to strengthen her mind and develop a down-to-earth, straightforward way of presenting beliefs that are often unorthodox but always profound. She tells it like it is!

"I don't care which spiritual path you follow, if at all," says Melanie. "I don't care where you've been, who you are, how much or how little experience or knowledge you think you have. I don't care who may have hurt you or how. There is always something more to be found within."

www.melaniehallett.com

The beliefs expressed in this book are those of the author.

CONTENTS

Introduction

Spiritualism is a way of life in which, as in other religions and philosophies, people try to better themselves through their awareness and beliefs. In particular, we don't 'live in hope' of an afterlife because the foundation of Spiritualism is mediumship – communication with spirit people. Mediums prove that life after death is real by demonstrating evidence of survival. We also communicate with spirit guides, enlightened souls who have moved into the next phase of life and who are able to advise us. They don't dictate to us, rather these people are there to help and it's like talking to a priest or a close friend about the best way to approach things.

People like me tend to be quite private about what we do as there is still a great deal of religious bigotry in the world and mediums get more than our fair share! This makes no sense when you think that over eighty per cent of the population report having had 'ghostly experiences'. It stuns me when I hear people tell of their encounters with spirit people and add "I know this sounds crazy…" What is insane is that people who have made absolutely no attempt to investigate the paranormal often make sweeping comments about people like me having to prove what I have experienced on a daily basis throughout my entire life. Perhaps they should prove that what I have seen is not true? My goodness, there is just so much evidence…

My grandmothers were mediums and my parents brought me up in a very spiritually open environment where being able to sense, see and hear spirit people was quite normal; indeed, it was accepted and nothing to get excited about. I was very lucky to have that freedom of spiritual expression. It meant that when I had a boyfriend who was also a medium, he was welcomed rather than rejected as he had been by his former girlfriend's parents. We married and I was brought happily into a world of psychic development; we had two sons, both of whom are also naturally mediumistic.

Since then, I have studied, meditated on, written about and worked within mediumship forever, or so it seems. There is very little I haven't seen but the more I learn, the more I know there is to learn. So I have also gained qualifications in various complementary therapies to supplement my healing work, though nowadays I specialise in trance mediumship.

As Spiritualism has no creed, we do have freedom of interpretation of the principles that we live by. These were handed down from the spirit world to us through mediumship and they offer us guidelines to live by: belief in a Divine Being, that we are one family of life, that we are all affected by how we behave towards others, that we alone are responsible for our own actions, that we are progressing spiritually and that we never die.

However, there are those who think that, even from a Spiritualist perspective, I am not normal. Indeed, many of the things I have witnessed are extreme. If you want to know the reality of human life, I am going to tell it like it is!

What I would like most of all from this little book is for you to find some guidance, or perhaps some comfort: you might just be having some or all of the same experiences as I shall describe so I want you to know that you are not alone – ever. There is always someone to hold your hand along this path in life and I extend you mine.

But I don't mind if I also disturb you a little, and make you think outside your comfort zone...

CHAPTER ONE

WHO AM I?

How do you define yourself? Suppose you are at a party and someone asks you your name and then what you do, which they always seem to, what do you say?

This is often a question that I try to avoid, as I am a medium (I talk to dead people) and a healer. Yes, like everyone else, I define myself by what I do and because what I do is seen in several different ways by different people – and some of those people might like to burn me at the stake – I am a bit careful about it. A lot of people find what I do fascinating, others find it completely boring, while a relatively small number think I'm evil although they don't really understand it at all. Admittedly, my job is weird stuff. Wouldn't you rather that people ask you what you like doing and what you don't? Perhaps that is far too personal and maybe they don't want you to ask them that question. Small talk environments can be so difficult, can't they?

I think that our past shapes our future and what or who we are now. The things that happen to us throughout childhood definitely influence who we see ourselves as being; perhaps we aren't that person at all but the stuff we've been through makes us think we are like that. Could it be also that those we mix with define us too? Of course it could.

Perhaps we also define ourselves by our memories, then. What are your first memories? I think I can remember my mother looking into my pram when I was a baby, but I've seen photographs of her doing that so perhaps my memory isn't what I think it is. The photograph might remind me of the experience or there may be no such early memory at all and I am merely being influenced by the future experience of looking at the photo. I have come to believe that the early memory was there from babyhood.

Now, I also have a vague memory of a man standing underneath the open tread staircase in the house my family lived in from my earliest years to the age of about two. I don't remember how he looked but I remember being scared – not of him, but of the stairs and that I might fall through them. This memory is much less tangible than the pram memory, perhaps because there is no photographic evidence to back it up. Looking at these memories, I believe that this is the very first time that a memory was imprinted into my head: the photographic evidence of Mum looking at me in my pram made the older me decide that this had definitely happened.

During anyone's lifetime, there must be thousands of times when we have come to believe something because there has been an apparently solid piece of evidence that has reinforced the concept. This is effectively indoctrination, something that we usually consider to be underhand and thoroughly nasty – a kind of brainwashing. But it happens absolutely every day when we look around, or listen to the radio, read a newspaper, watch TV or a film and when we read books, including ones that are thought to be holy. Ideas are reinforced until it becomes hard to say what we truly believe at all about something.

For example, when I was a kid my Mum was an avid Liberal and she used to rush around putting up orange 'Vote Liberal' signs. She was fond of saying things like "The country has gone to the dogs!" and being absolutely adamant that her political party would sort everything out. One of her deepest frustrations was coming across people, when she was canvassing door to door, who said that they were going to vote for another party "...because my Dad always did." She couldn't discuss it with them because many of them didn't actually have an opinion about politics or the economy. Many of the people she spoke to only voted the way they did because it was their 'family party'. This attitude also applies to religious views and even to where people buy their clothes! So many people identify themselves with the habits of their forebears: we have attitudes of mind that come from the social life around us and the beliefs and activities of our families.

We are also certain types of people because we inherit certain traits. I'm sure all parents can see the behaviour and attitudes of their own parents in themselves at times, for example when disciplining their kids, and we see our parents and grandparents within our children too. I know that I brought my sons up in exactly the same way and I have influenced their tastes for certain foods and activities. My parenting and the things around us in our lives have indoctrinated them into thinking in certain ways – and that can't be helped. It's not just all about the 'evil advertising agencies' and the violent computer games, the bullies at school and the pressure our kids are under to have certain material things like designer trainers.

And were we any different? Young people think that the previous generation knows nothing, has not experienced anything like they have and are so ancient they should be mummified. Goodness, all younger generations do that. When my eldest son grew his hair so long that he could sit on it, his Dad and I decided to pretend that we were shocked, hoping that this level of rebellion would be enough for him and it pretty much was. When he was older and woke up to the fact that Mum and Dad were cool – oh yeah – I told him about how I'd had blue hair and double ear piercings when I was a teenager, which was considered seriously wild at the time. And his Dad told him that his hair had been long and he'd had a seventies rock star perm and worn platform boots. Bootleg trousers were called flares and skinny jeans were called drain-pipes! What goes around comes around. The desire to wear fashionable clothes that follow the crowd, or the desire to be different, are all part of the suggestions that our world puts into people's heads as our Earthly lives progress. When these suggestions are repeated or emphasised, like the photo of me in the pram giving solidity to a faint memory, these thoughts all become part of who we think we are.

So if you were to meet me at a party and ask me who I am, I should probably say, "Hi, my name's Melanie. I teach spiritual development and I like music and staggering. That's my version of walking and does not involve alcohol or stimulants – I am disabled. I absolutely loathe rhubarb, both the kind that people eat and the kind that people speak."

It is when all those things that seem to define us fall away, that we find out who we are and who we are not. My struggles have helped me to see who I am not and what is left may be who I am; then I look at the leftovers time and time again, in contemplative meditation or during an intellectual rant over a cup of tea in the middle of the night. I truly believe that I know who I am right now but I may not know next week.

That's the first thing to understand about life. It ain't stable. It's not even hen house and it certainly ain't mansion-with-servants. Sorry for the terrible pun but it works. Stables and hen houses generally contain animals and a lot of poo that has to be cleaned out regularly. There are indeed many animals in life: nice ones, the furry, scaly and feathered types who are honest and simply the creatures that they are, and the other ones who have to put clothes on to keep warm. Yes, humans often behave like beasts and like to poo on other humans. And even that doesn't stay stable: sometimes the nice ones are nasty and shit happens and other times the nasty ones are nice and shit happens later.

A hen house tends to be small; it's where we live when we try and restrict our exposure to the world of unpleasantness. Here, we are no longer trying to go places, we have let go of the need to move on and we think we've found where we fit. We're cosy in our hen house, laying our own little eggs; perhaps it's the church we go to, or the club we've

joined, or the Neighbourhood Watch or the place of employment...
But when our little world turns upside down, we find that hens also
poo but can't fly.

At times, we might think that money and possessions will buy
happiness and we reach for the mansion-with-servants. We create our
special space and those who come into it must do as we want because
we're rich (or think we are). Perhaps our mansion is a business or a
place of employment where we're in a position of power. Perhaps it's
a spiritual or political centre where we are on the committee, or we're
even the leader, and we finally have power over others. Maybe, if it's
a spiritual place, we actually believe that what we are doing is for the
benefit of others. Then suddenly, someone who is not on our side or
on our committee refuses to do what we want or do things as we want
them done. We find that there is poo here too, because all humans
produce it. No amount of power or money brings happiness. Someone
will always make you fall off your perch.

Nothing is constant. Nothing stays in the same form. We are
shedding cells and skin and agility and years ahead of us, every single
moment of every day. People we love, die. People we don't love won't
leave. We die. The life we have at the moment comes to an end.
Everything changes into something else. When we burn wood it turns
into ashes. When we bury or cremate a body it converts into something
else too. The body passes away.

But there is a part of us that doesn't pass away and this part doesn't
answer the question "Who are you?" with a name, a job, hobbies and
dislikes.

And this is the real you.

Have you ever sat in meditation and found that you were looking back
at yourself, that you were observing yourself? Perhaps you have given
yourself a talking-to when something has upset you and realised that

it was as if you were talking to a third person. Again, in many of our dreams we watch ourselves having an experience and wonder if this is not really a dream... In these times, we are aware of our consciousness.

So we are not just the bag of bones we may think we are. When we die, the body does but this consciousness we have continues. This is often called 'life after death'. More people than not have experienced something they can't explain after a loved one has died. Clocks stop in the deceased person's home at the moment of death. People smell their grandmother's favourite scent or her fresh laundry straight from the line, when there is no-one there. They smell Dad's pipe tobacco during moments of distress or of joy, when he has long passed away and there is nothing that accounts for the fragrance. People just 'know' that their deceased loved one is present when strange coincidental things happen to remind them of that person: they turn on the radio on their Mum's birthday and find that her favourite song is being played right at that moment. And of course lots of people just simply 'see' their family member and have conversations with them on a regular basis. These people are called mediums, which is just a term for someone who perceives dead people, animals or another dimension of life.

I am a medium and I always have been one. I was born this way and it is something that runs in my family. I have the ability to communicate with other dimensions of life. I can hear, see and feel people who have passed on and even be aware of fragrances that are transmitted to my mind from these people. Just as we have senses that we use in this dimension to communicate with one another, mediums use the same senses but attuned to another dimension – like being tuned into a different radio station. The things that I am writing about in this book are my own experiences as a medium, a healer and a psychic. Perhaps you have had similar experiences and maybe you are aware that you are psychic and would like to understand more. I hope that my words will help you to understand your own abilities.

Mediumship and many other psychic abilities are natural to all humans and animals. Some people are gifted with the ability and are able to do a great deal with it while others have a little flicker of it. Not everyone is born a Mozart: some of us can only manage Chopsticks while others can just about bang a key on a piano with one finger. As in all things, there are levels of skill and some have a capacity that seems to be outside of the norm.

Lots of people in the West have forgotten about their psychic abilities, such as knowing that something is going to happen (premonition) or that they can communicate with their ancestors. This was something that was normal in the more ancient civilisations of Europe but first orthodox religion crushed that and then science decreed that it was unprovable nonsense. It rapidly became dangerous to be psychic. You were burned at the stake, or ducked on the ducking stool and only considered innocent of witchcraft if you drowned. And of course the more ancient pagan ways of life, such as the Craft and Druidism, were seen as the work of the Devil, he being a myth created by orthodox religion to frighten people into submission and to obey the will of the Church. Later, in the early Victorian days for example, if you happened to be a scientist who investigated Spiritualism it is highly likely that you would be drummed out of every professional scientific body, lose your job and perhaps even be beaten up. Yes, scientists were literally beaten up; so it is no wonder they were a bit nervous about looking into the occult (which just means 'hidden things').

It is fascinatingly sad to see how the ignorant control so many others, or to watch those with intelligent psychic abilities allowing themselves to be controlled. There are numerous books and essays on the persecution of psychics but this one is not designed for that – there is quite enough negativity in the world already without making you feel rotten and cross whilst reading about it, so let's move on to happier things.

When we die, our bodies lose their animating force. Ha, maybe that doesn't sound too happy, talking about death, but isn't it good news to know that this is not the end? If you have had the difficult experience of being with someone when they have died, you will have witnessed the life force leave the body. The body becomes empty, devoid of life. But then the person moves out of the body and returns to the non-physical form that they were before the body was created. We are the animating force that makes our bodies function. Think of your body as your car – which is pretty cool as it does all the things you need it to do – while the real you, the part of you that you may have spotted from time to time looking on, is the driver. You are not your body; that's just the vehicle you use to manoeuvre around the Earth.

Now, this next bit might freak you out a bit, but hang in there. It is we ourselves who created our bodies, our vehicles. The part of us that made our bodies is the part that is conscious of 'all that is', for we are spiritual beings in a material form at the moment. We don't become spiritual beings when the body dies for we already are that; we have placed our limitless consciousness into a limited form for a while. Let this thought stew a bit...

The mind is not confined to the brain. I know this from experience and here are some stories to illustrate it. There are many instances of people having out-of-body experiences (OBEs) when having surgery, or near-death experiences (NDEs). My second husband was seriously injured some years ago and 'died' twice on the operating table. He talks about how he was surrounded by light when he died and there were several very tall, glowing figures surrounding him on the operating table. He saw himself outside his own body and watching these glowing 'angels', as he called them, fixing him. He says that he was then told by God to "Go back" because he was needed.

Jan was a dear friend of mine who has now passed on; she told me about how she had a heart attack and 'died'. She was also in a light-filled place and glowing figures offered her a beautiful, shining gown to wear. She was told that if she put the gown on she would not be able to go back, but that if she did go back to Earth she would be seriously impaired physically. Jan felt that she couldn't leave her husband, so she rejected the gown and allowed herself to be resuscitated. Notice her choice of language: she 'allowed herself' because she had a choice.

My Dad had a heart attack when I was very young and he collapsed onto the soft grass in the garden. He was terrified of dying. He told me later that he saw his own long-dead father standing with his mother, even longer-dead, at the end of a light-filled tunnel. He was shooting along it and his parents told him, without words, that he could go back if he wanted to. So Dad put the brakes on with his knees and elbows against the side of the light tunnel and woke up in hospital. There were grazes on his knees and elbows, consistent with his braking in the tunnel, but not consistent with his fall or anything that he had been doing that day. Hmm, thought-provoking, eh?

One of the things that mediums and psychics do is meditate. There are different types of meditation that can be used, ranging from a style where the object is to clear the mind and become still through to a more directed focus, often used in Spiritualism specifically to communicate with people in the spirit world. In some forms of meditation it is usual for the meditator to see all sorts of wonderful things, or to hear and feel all sorts of wonderful things, or both. One can literally feel that one has left the body, losing all awareness of it and shooting off into outer space. During the Cold War in Europe, Russian and American psychics were taught to do this and to travel to a specific place, remotely viewing areas that their government considered to be a threat such as missile silos or fuel dumps. Psychics do this quite naturally; but it doesn't feel very nice if you are forcing yourself to go somewhere guarded or secret.

What remote viewing and near-death experiences show is that the mind is not confined to the brain. The brain is like the engine of our car and the driver is our mind. The mind is not a simple thing; I never thought humans were simple, did you?

So, let's ask the question again. Who are you? Well, you are human but you are not confined to your body and you will live on after death.

CHAPTER TWO

THE PURPOSE OF LIFE

Does there need to be a purpose? Is it arrogant to think we're important enough to have a purpose? Is my purpose any more important than yours, if I even have one? In Buddhism, people are encouraged to detach from emotion and craving and just to 'be'.

I used to find it terribly frustrating at school when the Science teacher couldn't give me a reason for chemical reactions. She would say, "This is just what happens." Then I was always in detention at the Roman Catholic convent school that I went to in Brussels when I asked things like, "If God created everything, who created God?" Again, there was no answer. In many religions, it is said that God is 'unknowable' and, in Christianity particularly, we are encouraged to believe that it is God's will whether things are done or not done. There is the 'things happen just because they do' answer again.

Many of us spend much of this life trying to work out why we are here. I have come to realise that the question I was really asking was, "Am I important?" I was looking for a sense of self-importance amid the hurly burly of human life, looking for some self-esteem; and as soon as I found it, something would happen to take it away again.

Now, I'm not talking about silly little things where I threw my rattle out of the pram. My life so far has been pretty difficult: I have been sexually, mentally and physically abused from birth.[1] So I can't help wondering about the purpose of life. Well, I have learned about compassion, patience, reliability and kindness from these things – sometimes my experiences of them and sometimes someone else's, sometimes my lack and sometimes someone else's lack.

But what hits me square on the chin is that emotions and things like self-esteem or indeed anything to do with the 'self' are totally transient, limited and an illusion. If they were solid, limitless and real, these feelings would remain with me – but they don't. They don't now and they won't when I die. I realised that I could feel tremendously self-aware, comfortable with my behaviour, joyful and peaceful one minute – and then someone would say something or I would be reminded of a horrible event that occurred years ago and wham, I would lose all that and be somewhere else instead. Equally, I could be totally fed up, almost suicidal, directionless and terrified one minute and the next minute a dear friend would ring me and tell me that they love me and they called because they felt I was miserable and wham, I would lose all that and be somewhere else instead again.

Emotions and the feelings that belong to this individualised self, this person that one appears to be at the moment, are not real or solid or fixed and there is really no point in building one's life around them. Of course, it is important to behave well, which means causing no harm to anyone if we can help it. We must do our best to be as harmless as possible to all life, including the creatures that share this world with us, and of course as harmless as possible to the planet herself. The key is to do one's best. I think the phrase 'Do unto others as you would be done by' is perfect because it's true on so many levels. On the one hand, you would really hate it if someone were cruel to you, so put yourself in their shoes and don't be cruel to them; and on the other hand, when you harm another you are harming yourself anyway, as We Are One.

[1] If you ever want to hear about it and only because you think it might help you, then ask me; but I don't see the need to go over it all time and time again.

12

There is a state of detachment that is a good thing to aim for in our head and heart. It's not a cold place to be. It is a place where we don't attack the person who is horrid to us but we can defend ourselves; it's not spiritual to get battered by someone and they won't learn to be nice if they get away with their bad behaviour. Equally, if we were to be violently horrible back, all we are doing is doubling up the darkness. There's a happy medium to be found, somewhere in the middle between lying down and getting kicked and smacking them in the face. We have to measure each situation individually and if we are detached from the immediate emotion that pain causes, then we won't just react in a knee-jerk style, we will act with more consideration and love. May I repeat, it is not spiritual to allow oneself to be a punch bag. We are then excluding someone from the unconditional love that we are trying to live within. We are excluding ourselves too. And we can love someone from our higher self even if we are having a hard time doing anything other than hating them from our Earthly individual self.

So, given these illusions, is there a purpose in life? Well, yes. The purpose is just to be and to accept that as a species of creatures we incarnate onto planets. We are a limitless Being that breaks itself into smaller parts, or so it seems, and has a go at living a limited life in a body that decays and dies, forgets what it is almost completely, and strives to love all the other parts like it did when it was One. Or, think of it this way: we are like a butterfly that goes through various forms of life but is still a butterfly. Life just is. That's how it is.

In moments of spiritual liberation – or enlightenment, if you prefer that word – there is a clear knowing of this. There is absolute certainty that everything is as it's meant to be, that we are both tiny and apparently insignificant and limitless and extremely important all at the same time. There is absolute love without question and a feeling of such peace and security that we just can't believe it until we feel it. And I hope you will.

Our purpose in life is also what we make it. In our efforts to understand why we are here, we analyse our skills and then try to use them to make other people's suffering lessen. Mediums, for example, try to alleviate the grief of bereavement by bringing communication from souls who have moved on into the next phase of life. They are still butterflies, just out of the body, that's all. They are actually part of one mind, one being, and we communicate with one another telepathically all of the time. It is so normal that we barely notice.

Mediums, healers and others on a spiritual or vocational pathway, often ask if what happens here on the Earth is important to the spirit world, to our guides and also to God. Looking at our loved ones who have passed over into the spirit world first, it is of course still important to our parents and grandparents and those who have loved us when they were alive here on Earth that we are safe, loved and happy. Even though We Are One, when we incarnate we are all trapped within this individualisation of the spirit, the sense of self. Your Grandma is still your Grandma, as each time she connects mentally to anyone on the Earth her memories of being your Grandma are to the forefront, and she will respond accordingly directly with you through your own mediumistic awareness or via another medium. Moreover, some spirit people remain in this 'vibration', as it were attached to the Earth plane; they are not tied down here through anything we have done, nor are they prevented from moving on, but the sense of self is what the Earth plane says to us as we draw close to it. There is a mental sphere of Earthly knowledge and experience that we tap into, making us remember who we are.

In many religious cultures, people are encouraged to 'go into the Light' when they die, so that they move away from this sense of self and become at one with 'all that is'. Yet the experiences we have here leave a huge and frequently indelible mark and it is hard to become a free spirit again. This is why some mediums and healers spend time 'moving people on' once they have died and also why there are hauntings and recurring memories stuck in certain locations.

I have often asked my guides about the vocational path I follow, asking if I'm going the right way or meant to be doing this or that, and they usually answer in a silent way, with a feeling of love or warmth. White Owl, a Lakota gentleman long in the spirit world, usually asks me a question in return when I ask him things like this. My response is, "Oh, so you're doing the psychoanalysis thing, then, answering my question with a question?" He always laughs, not in a condescending way but just because he has a wicked sense of humour, which he recalls from his last incarnation here. When pressed during one of my many rough times in life, he told me that he was not remotely bothered whether I work spiritually or not. I was shocked, as I'm sure many other mediums and spiritual workers would be, and I asked him why this was so. Here is his answer:

> "Mediumship is not the path to enlightenment, which if I had to wish for something for you, is what I would wish for. When enlightened and awake spiritually, it becomes clear that the psychic and spiritual abilities are merely bi-products of walking the spiritual path. Being able to talk with me does not make you filled with unconditional love. Being able to bring proof of the continuance of life beyond material death may bring a sense of comfort to a bereaved or curious person, but it does not set them on the path to enlightenment unless that person is prepared to look beyond the material plane and see their wholeness.

> "When I speak of 'wholeness', I am talking about the complete being that you are. You are not an individual. You are part of something so much greater, so much larger. Every aspect of your being – your body, your mind, your soul – is the body, mind and soul of all life. There is no separation between you and all that lives, all that is.

> "If you would call that God, Great Spirit or whatever you like,

it doesn't matter, as long as you realise that it's not a man on a cloud with a flowing white beard. There is no He, She or even It, nor is it Them. All that is, is literally that; and the capacity that you and many like you have to talk to people (because I am a person, just a dead one) is the same capacity you have to communicate with all minds and all life.

"Instead of spending time honing your gift to communicate with the spirit world, spend time developing the ability to hear your higher self sing. At this moment and in all moments, you are in full communication with all life. This is all that ever has been, all that is and all that will ever be. There is no start or stop for this, it all just is.

"If mankind could communicate with every creature and life form, it is highly likely that it would stop killing them as men would realise that this is futile. What is the point in killing yourself over and over again?

"Your job is to work in the way that is right for you at this present time. It is very hard to fully understand what at-one-ment is when living in the delusion of the Earth plane. But that's part of the way, to be able to live universally despite feeling individual. At the moment, you are being the best you can be and doing the best that you can; so in that way, yes, it is right for you to be working in the way that you are. However, the day will come when this will change and we will need to speak of this again. Not for me to tell you what to do, but for you to tell me what you would like me to do."

"...that's part of the way, to be able to live universally despite feeling individual."

And he was right. That day did come. Everything changes.

Perhaps one of the reasons that we start along this path of spiritual enquiry is because something happens so that the way we thought we were walking clearly and happily along suddenly stops. Usually this is something dreadful. Is that what drew you to it? I have done the opposite at times as I have always been on this path; I grew up with it and talking to dead people is normal for me, but religion is not. I guess I found religion when I found God and I needed a place to research that in.

I have been deeply hurt along my pathway of unfoldment and, surprisingly, by people who are supposed to be spiritual; that drove me away from the religious path again. I couldn't understand how those who were supposed to be running Spiritualism could allow such dreadful behaviour. Wasn't there some sort of punishment system, such as defrocking, in Spiritualism? Yes there is, but spiritual people don't like confrontation and don't like looking at nasty stuff. And no-one likes to accept that there is bad behaviour in the gang they belong to because it looks bad for them too, doesn't it?

I had really thought that my purpose for living was to be a medium and to help people, but now I know that it isn't. Being a medium, a healer or spiritual worker of any kind and in any walk of life or religion, is no better than any other job. What is important is the way we do our jobs. Or if we are out of work or unable to work, the way we handle that is just as important in the grand scheme of things as being Prime Minister or King or Archbishop. It is all about mindfulness and doing our living in a way such that we get absolutely everything out of it we can, to be a kinder and more loving, more supportive person. You can be Chancellor of the Exchequer with the potential to ease child poverty and instead filch the money for those who are already rich. You can be a refuse collector yet help disabled people by collecting their bins from the back of the house and then taking them back again. You can be a priest and abuse children, or a church warden who maintains all the graves in your own time just so that the bereaved relatives are uplifted. There is an opportunity to be a complete arse in every aspect of life – or to be an angel.

I am fortunate to be one of those people who have clear memories of other incarnations I have had. I used to talk to my parents about this as a two-year old and I was able to talk about historical events hundreds of years previously and way beyond a child's knowledge. This is my experience and these memories have allowed me to connect with many of my own 'soul group' members. A soul group is a collection of spirit people with whom you incarnate a lot, and you are attracted to each other in order to experience certain things in life. It's a bit like being molecules that quite like each other and are drawn together to make something.

Having this knowledge has helped me to understand the purpose of life a little better and I would like to share that with you because I suspect that many of you will have this awareness too. I noticed that I was repeating things in my life, often. Now, I know about learned behaviour and how we humans learn by repetition, but this was nuts. It was like I was re-dancing the same dance over and over again; the same kind of people would keep turning up to splatter me and then someone else similar would do the same. It became really ridiculous when even their names were the same too. It was like some bright spark up in Heaven was pressing the rewind button all the time. Know that one? I then noticed that all of a sudden a situation would stop repeating but there was a feeling of release in the pit of my stomach.

Then I found more and more people whom I recognised in a kind of deja-vu way, and these people also recognised me even though I deliberately didn't say anything. All of these people had a particular memory from Bhutan and all had been monks; we had all died violently, apart from a handful of boy monks who remembered the slaughter too and actually felt guilty for not dying. It got seriously out of hand as I met more and more of these people and they were still troubled by the past life and were all devoted servants of God.

A group of about a dozen of these people became very close friends and I found that we were all dealing with the same issues, mainly abandonment and persecution. It was happening to us over and over again.

We looked at our childhoods and found that we had all experienced abuse. We found so many likenesses that it was way past coincidence. For example, we even lived within a few miles of each other yet had all been born in different parts of the country. Spooky is the word.

As I was close to them all, I knew what they were dealing with at any given time and something amazing began to happen. When an issue that another soul group member faced was resolved, an almost identical issue was dealt with by me too – yet I didn't have to do anything at all. It just got sorted and I saw this happen for the others as well. I was astonished. I watched this for several years and, yes, it happened a lot.

After a while I noticed a shift inside me and now I feel that I know when one of us has completed something and I believe that we are working very much as a team. I also realised that these experiences were therefore not personal: I didn't have to resolve something because as long as one of my soul group members did so, and we all completed different parts of the puzzle, then the puzzle was done. It had nothing to do with any misdemeanours I might have been guilty of (though of course, if I did something dreadful then this would affect the rest of my soul group too).

This helped me to understand that, truthfully, as we are told in so many holy books and by so many inspiring teachers in all sorts of religious pathways, that what we do to others affects us and, of course, what we learn and improve upon affects everyone too. Be bad and everyone gets hurt. Be good and everyone gets hugged. Naturally, we don't often realise this because we're too busy thinking that we are separate. But this realisation has helped me to know, by experience, that we really aren't apart at all.

When we have an experience, pleasant or otherwise, we have the opportunity of being absorbed into that experience. We can flick our eyes over it and barely give it a thought, or we can really scrutinise it and know it. It's hard to be that mindful but, if we try, we can reduce our need to look repeatedly at issues and thereby reduce the need for the rest of our soul group to look again and again.

So our purpose in life is just to experience everything that life on Earth can offer within the boundaries of the things we elected to investigate when we incarnated. We'll look at 'life choices' a bit more later on.

CHAPTER THREE

THE MATERIAL
AND SPIRITUAL REALMS

During many years involved in Spiritualism, I have been taught that the Earth plane is a heavy place filled with suffering and that when I pass over I will be pain-free and living in a peaceful place. I will be able to review my Earthly life and judge myself, then naturally gravitate to a suitable level of living and will be compensated or receive retribution for all my good and evil deeds. In Spiritualism it is believed that God does not judge us, rather we judge ourselves.

It has become very clear to me that an awful lot of Spiritualists, and other people on a spiritual path who prefer not to be labelled but call themselves 'spiritual' (and a lot of them are indeed very spiritual people, in the sense that they try hard to be kind), really do believe that the Earth is almost a punishment. They speak of 'lessons' that they must learn here and say that everything will make more sense once we are back in 'the world of spirit'.

But the thing is – we are already in the world of spirit. There is nowhere that is not the world of spirit.

Spiritualism teaches that we are spirit here and now, yet there is this mixed-up idea that we are somehow only 'true spirit beings' once we have snuffed it. This is simply not true. We are indeed spirit here and now and being dead doesn't turn people into enlightened creatures who know everything. We already know everything.

This life is not a time of punishment. Yes, it is a place of learning, but all dimensions of life are that. And lessons aren't always hard-learned, achievements aren't always hard-won. This is orthodoxy speaking, indoctrination that has seeped into our society and into the ways of thinking that we are drawn to.

In some cultures it is believed that when we reincarnate, having been really naughty, our punishment is to be an animal of some kind and the naughtier we have been the more lowly the animal. Well, I reckon it would be quite cool to spend a life as a mayfly – kind of a short life, but still cool as lives go. And if I could be a spoilt pussy cat like the cats I have loved… well, I'm purring already. I can understand the life of an ox pulling an overladen cart and being beaten with a bamboo cane as suffering, but there are thousands of humans who are overworked, starved and beaten. I wonder which animal is being punished for a badly led past life by being made to become a rotten human? My suggestion is that a lot of humans are far more unpleasant than animals.

So, material life is spiritual in nature in that it affords us many opportunities to develop our knowledge and to share that with all life. (Many believe that we do that when we are asleep.) It might be better to think of this life we are living as being just one step in a much longer journey. Our opportunities should not be belittled and our life is not something to be endured before our happy times being dead. We are capable of such awareness and unconditional love right here and now.

Time is a concept that we only have in this material life. We are born, we live and we pass away. We have a beginning, a middle and an end – or so we think – because right now we are unable to look beyond the self. We think that we are individuals and we are unable to conceive of the totality, the wholeness of life, in the state of consciousness we are in here. Yet we can perceive that wholeness in deep meditation and sometimes in flashes of enlightenment. If we take away this idea of beginning and ending, we come to a state of being where there is no such concept of time. All ancient spiritual cultures tell us that life is a circle, the Medicine Wheel, a circular pattern. The human race has done living before. We have expanded and contracted, we have flowed along a path that has apparently concluded and then started again. When we die – we don't. We just move into another state of consciousness.

I have been fortunate enough to communicate with many other 'me's. Moving into an unusual mental state, I have become one with my higher self and have stepped into other facets of my existence. I am not alone in this, many other people have done this too. The interesting thing is that I seemed to occupy the same point in space and time and yet also didn't occupy any space or time. I just was. I think that it is possible to be a future self and perhaps this is how some people are able to tell the future. I know that this happens to me though it is something that I don't seek; it just comes from 'knowing', which is a kind of clairvoyance that is natural to a less structured self (being less Earthly and therefore less tied down to the concepts that we associate with solidity and being human). The knowing comes to me in very clear thoughts that I hear; but the voice is not mine, does not belong to any of the spirit guides I know, is always the same voice, and is absolutely right every single time. Sometimes it can take years for the truth of this knowing to become apparent, but it always has done.

The idea of being able to communicate with future 'me's might suggest that everything is written in advance and that we have no free will, but I don't believe that to be true. It comes down again to this concept of solidity that being an individualised spirit brings, this idea that everything follows a time line, usually with us being the kingpin. However, as time is an idea that only works here, and because absolutely everything is changing all the time, because that's its natural state, then why should our future selves remain in what we think of as a static position? I am changing all the time, so therefore the other 'me's, including my past, are also changing because change is the natural state, flow is the natural state. There is no stagnation, no sitting still, nothing stays the same. It's not meant to and part of the lesson of the Earthly life is to understand that. White Owl, one of my dear guides, loves the phrase 'Go with the flow' – very apt here. The world is flowing and moving all the time. We are moving at about 600 mph at this moment, sitting in our chairs, yet we think we're still. We don't realise that we're moving because our speed is relative to what's going on around us. If a bird flies past the window, it appears to be flying faster than we are sitting, of course.

Relativity is highly relevant to spiritual understanding, because We Are One. This is why we all see trees as trees, the sky as the sky and people as people; we are one mind, a collective consciousness perceiving everything. As a species, we like to gather together and we particularly like gathering together with others who see things in the same way that we do. (This has been called a 'node'.) Once enough of us believe something, we create a critical mass and suddenly we all believe it. If enough of us run round screaming "Fire!", pretty much everyone will soon be running around screaming "Fire!" and believing that there is a fire. It is the same concept as the soul group described earlier, a node of spirits who are drawn together time and time again; and the more we draw together the more the connection is solidified.

I remember being in the street once in London and a couple of lads started looking up at the skyline, at the edge of a roof. Within five minutes, a crowd of people was looking up and searching for the person who was about to jump until eventually the lads laughed, said "Gullible" and walked off. There was no-one up on the roof.

We all need to view the world as one mind. If enough people could do this, we would lose the misperception that we are individuals and potentially this would end all wars, famine and general injustice in the world. Once you realised that everyone is you, who in their right mind would hurt themselves? On the other hand, perhaps we need some parts of humanity that apparently just can't come together, so that the collective can have the full experience of non-collectiveness?

So, all dimensions of life are spiritual in nature and it is important to understand what the word 'spiritual' means here. It is not about being nice, but simply about being spirits – beings who continue past Earthly death, multi-dimensional and limitless creatures.

Some years ago, while I was meditating, happily sitting in silence and watching my breath, White Owl appeared in my mind and I found myself standing in front of him. We smiled at each other because we love each other very much, and then he took my hand and led me to a dugout canoe bobbing about at the edge of a beautiful river. He helped me into the canoe. As he did so, I saw my legs and realised that I was wearing a light-coloured, flowing dress that seemed to glow. I accepted this at the time as being totally normal; well, what else would you wear when going boating with your spirit guide? He untied the canoe and pushed away with a paddle and off we went downstream. No words were spoken at this point.

The river water became gradually thicker, maybe like syrup or clear glue. It reminded me of ectoplasm, the substance used in séance rooms for the production of physical phenomena like transfiguration or the materialisation of spirit people. (More about that later.) As I looked ahead to where we were going, I saw that the river flowed into the side of a mountain. We entered this and I was a little perturbed as I am claustrophobic and lygophobic (frightened of the dark). Then immediately the river began to glow with a gentle mixture of colours and I could see quite clearly.

After a while, we came into an enormous cavern. I couldn't see the edges of it, but I felt excited and tremendously safe. White Owl asked me mentally if I would like to "…enter the water." I knew by now that this stuff was not water (but I'll call it that for now) and looked at him with trepidation as I'm also not good in water (aquaphobic!), so he calmly slipped over the side of the canoe and held out his hand. I saw that he wasn't wet and so I slipped in too – in a far more ladylike way than I could ever manage when in my physical body. That made me laugh, then the water rippled as I laughed and seemed to be laughing too. It was like being in a high salt bath. I didn't sink down very deep and I didn't have to tread water, I was just held there. Then I felt something touch me, though not with a hand; it was a gentle connection just like when a spirit person touches one's mind. Out of the water rose my Granddad and then my Nan came out too. I was very moved, watching as they formed themselves from the water.

Suddenly I was aware of so many thoughts of love, friendship and recognition as my mind filled with memories of times that I had spent with my grandparents. White Owl told me now that I could know all memories and there, right in front of me, he melted into the water. Without worrying about it, I did the same. I didn't need to be told how to, I just knew how and melted into it too, there in the cavern.

One word came into my mind: 'Nirvana'. This is a Buddhist term that describes a transcendent state of consciousness where all pain, desire and self is gone. There is no longer any karma – or in Spiritualist terms, compensation and retribution for all good and evil deeds done on Earth – and there is no rebirth. It is called Moksha in Hinduism and Jainism. We don't really have an English word for it. Losing one's sense of self is quite difficult for us in the West as we have been taught to be quite self-conscious. Many people are now spending a fortune trying to lose that awareness of self, because we equate it with ego and egocentricity (which is false).

I have no idea how long I was within the water in the cavern but when I came to I felt bereft, so alone. I had 'gone home', being at one with all that is. It was a different experience to other times when I had been 'within God', and it had moved me deeply.

Thinking about this experience later, I understand the river to be 'the flow' that White Owl talks about so much, an energy that encapsulates all life and all time, a formless flow that we live in all the time. There is a definite current to it, a definite mind, and the various coloured lights that had lit my way to the cavern had come alive because the flow knew that I was there and knew my fear. Other minds there understood because they had known it too, and none of the experiences that any of the minds had had were distinct. When I was in there, I wasn't me, there was no 'I'. There was just being. Oneness.

This experience had a profound effect on me for days afterwards. I have returned there many times and it is rejuvenating! I understand from it that this life really is illusory, as mystics over time have told us. There are no separate dimensions or realms at all and no separate people, not on a fundamental level of life.

Sorry to say it again, but We Are One.

CHAPTER FOUR

WHAT IS LIFE?

I suppose we are asking two things here. Does being alive mean having sentience and a sense of self? Sentience is about feeling and usually that means having emotions or feeling pain. The second question about what constitutes life is whether there are degrees of awareness. A dog is alive but it can't do algebra (but then who wants to?).

Another way at looking at this is how we as a species perceive life. What do we feel when we interact with animals? Is there an exchange of ideas or emotions? It's one thing to anthropomorphise animals, dress them in little jackets and hats in children's story books and on television, but it's another to sense recognition and acknowledge that an animal perceives us and can communicate with us, because of course they can. Any pet owner will say that as will most psychics. Frankly, those who don't think that animals are sentient are crackers.

When I was a kid I used to play with my teddy bears and they would answer me back, just like other kids' do, especially desperately lonely ones like me. Many of the answers Ted gave me weren't coming from his straw-stuffed head, of course; they were coming from my higher self, personified (or is that teddified?) in my toy, and also from my guides. I was also able to chat with my guides in their more usual form as floaty dead people, but sometimes only Ted's wisdom would help. He even had his own passport as my family travelled an awful lot, and it had to be stamped by patient Border Agency officers. Well, I was very sweet and pretty.

However, inanimate objects like teddies can take on an energy from the mind and become, effectively, idols. This is of course banned in the Bible as Paganism and other ancient religions used statues to remind them of their deity. Any idol, statue, crystal or other object treated with reverence, say in a medicine bundle or on an altar, holds a kind of life of its own; but there's no real mind within it, just echoes of the thoughts, feelings and activities of those who handle it. In psychometry, a sensitive reads these energy signatures left within objects.

Animals

Animals of all kinds – fish, birds, mammals, reptiles – have awareness of self. They have a hierarchical society too, a pecking order if you like. They communicate from the spirit world just as humans do and they behave in ways that will blow your mind, if you watch them carefully.

When I was about eight years old, my family lived in a very haunted farmhouse in Essex. Everything about the atmosphere of the house and grounds was different, heightened, as if 'something' were brewing and had also brewed over. My parents both had mothers who were mediums and the ability is well and truly established throughout the generations. So we stimulated spooky energy. Our pets were also very psychic, which of course is just as natural for them as it is for us, and we had very close relationships with one another.

One day I skipped along from seeing my Godparents who lived next door, passing through a little avenue of overhanging weeping willow, walnut and cherry trees, towards the laundry room door to our house, obscured by the drooping branches. I froze with fascination due to the scene unfolding before me. Noddy, my big ginger tomcat with eight toes on his front feet and seven on his back ones, was sitting slap bang in the middle of the path with chest puffed out and eyes bright, looking just like a lion. From my right came Blinky, the smaller cat with normal paws, being pushed towards Noddy by Inky, the middle-sized cat with seven toes on her front feet and six on the back. Inky was pushing her in the rear with her head.

Blinky came to a halt in front of Noddy with Inky at her side. She hung her head. Noddy and Inky looked into each other's eyes for some time and I could feel that there was communication happening. Then Inky looked down as if bowing. Noddy now looked at Blinky who lifted her head and they looked into each other's eyes too before Blinky dropped her head again. Noddy brought up his huge paw and whacked her round the head. She slunk off. Noddy and Inky seemed to talk again mentally. Inky left the way she had come as Noddy sat still for a while and looked at me. He had allowed me to watch. Finally he got up and walked off in the opposite direction. The atmosphere was highly charged during this exchange; it reminds me now of the sense of anticipation when physical phenomena are about to happen in a séance room.

Here were three cute, fluffy pussy cats with soppy names, but that was no cuddly experience. It was three animals in court, with deliberation, judgement passed and punishment meted. Some code had been violated. There was intelligence and a sense of right and wrong and of self.

I was told by the late Don Galloway that it was not good practice in mediumship to give communication from spirit animals; rather, one should ask a spirit person to bring an animal if it wished to bring a message to a loved one on Earth. He said that this was to appease the people outside the movement who found communication with spirit people hard enough – chats with animals would be too much for them. I tried very hard to follow that advice, but with my experience over the years and following much delving into Earth-based religions like Shamanism, I now just give the thoughts of a communicating animal as it comes. It's about time that humans understood that animals have feelings too.

However, there are places where giving animal messages is a bit dodgy, to say the least, and that's usually in starchy, rule-based Spiritualist churches. There I was in a starchy, rule-based Spiritualist church in the Midlands. The chairperson was the President and had a dreadful reputation for being a tartar. I had demonstrated in the toughest Spiritualist venues in the UK, with congregations filled with the most difficult of members such as other mediums with ego problems, so I was fairly comfortable. I compensated for the judgmental attitude that oozed from the lady and her church with lots of smiles and love. So imagine my horror, after several by-the-book messages involving just normal dead people, when a cow appeared at the back of the church…

Now, this was a really clear clairvoyant image. She walked down the aisle, swishing her tail, and I ignored her. I struggled to give another message to someone else and she became clearer and clearer. I could smell her. I could feel the softness of her fur and then she let out an enormous "Moo!" I jumped and decided, what the hell, to go for it. They probably wouldn't invite me again anyway as I had laughed too much during the service. The cow sent her thoughts to me and it was just the same in my head as when a spirit human thinks to me. Unless clairaudience is involved, when one actually hears words or sounds, what happens is that the mind creates words to use, just as it does when one expresses one's own thoughts. It's all a very natural process. I had heard the moo clairaudiently, but the cow's thoughts were inside my mind.

She wanted me to give her message to the chairperson. Oh, what a nightmare! The cow told me her name was Daisy. Of course, what else could it have been – maybe Ermintrude, with a daisy in her mouth like in The Magic Roundabout? And yes, she really did have a daisy in her mouth and appeared to be chewing the cud.

Her story was heart-breaking. She said that the chairperson had grown up on a farm, that Daisy's mother had died giving birth to her and the lady had hand-reared her. When Daisy was older and had had a calf herself, the chairperson had begged her father not to take it away, but he had and Daisy had cried for ages. The lady had comforted her and she never had another calf. She lived out her life as the lady's friend and pet and, of course, not as a milk cow. The chairperson confirmed all this and began to smile (which was a very rare thing). Then Daisy told me that the lady had been in love, had fallen pregnant but had lost her baby, and that her lover had died in World War II. She had never married and had been sad her whole life. Now Daisy had come to support her and to tell her that she was loved and that, when she died, her lover and Daisy would be there to meet her. The chairperson cried buckets. She passed over to spirit not long after this.

So, here we have an animal communicating compassion and understanding through a shared experience. This cow is clearly conscious of herself, knows grief and knows that human beings suffer in the same way. There was no spirit human with me or Daisy when this message was relayed. This tells me very clearly that animals are sentient.

Humans

There are just too many experiences of life after death regarding humans for us not to know that life is continuous. To all those who disagree, I say you haven't been looking in the right places, nor have you experienced enough in life. I'm not going to waste my time talking about it because the knowledge is right in front of our faces. People don't die. Life is continuous. Humans are definitely alive all the time, even when they're dead!

Angels

One of my early teachers called them ANcillary Guardians of the Environment of Life, which he took from an old science fiction radio show, though it's a good description. 'Ancillary' means providing necessary support to the activities or operation of an organisation or system, and this is something that they do.

They aren't human and never have been, but humans can aspire to be like an angel. Some Spiritualist organisations say that angels are just something that orthodox Christianity created in order to explain spirit manifestations and to control the experiences that their followers actually had. The wings are said just to be an aura. However, once you've met an angel you will disagree wholeheartedly with that. I am fortunate to have had many encounters with Archangel Michael, who oversees my soul group, and I am guided by an angel called Lana. (Hey, don't freak out about that – I've just told you that I talk to dead cows!)

Sometimes Michael presents himself as the most enormous chap you've ever seen and other times he's simply a feeling of soft love. Then again he can be so powerful that he's scary, but he's totally safe unless I mess up… he doesn't punish me, he wouldn't, but he's really good at showing me how I've messed up and the effect I've had on others by being so stupid. He's also really good at scooping me up when I feel useless.

As far as I am aware, Lana has only guided me and one other person, but she has also guided me previously when I was someone else. I'll let you run that through your head for a while. I was then a nun on the Isle of Iona and she drew close to me when I was sitting in a meadow meditating. She's also huge and not huge at times, bright and very powerful but never scary.

Lots of people have had experiences with angels. There are numerous books on the subject and there is almost a cult building up around it. Personally, when a subject becomes so overly organised in someone's head that they decide to write rules and instructions on how to communicate with a particular type of being, or on how to acquire certain gifts, that's the time I move away. You can't apply left brain ideas to right brain experiences.

Angels are real, they can go anywhere, they don't die and are almost sort of alien really, but they're beautiful and beneficent. Oh, and they don't fall from Heaven or from grace. Lucifer, the Devil, is a mythological creature made up by orthodox Christians long ago in an attempt to destroy the old ways, the old Earth-based religions. The Church decided to turn Hern the Hunter, Pan, the Green Man or Cernunnos into something nasty; these gods had horns, so the Devil was created with horns to frighten and control the early Christians. Of course, just like my teddy bear and idols: the fear, judgement and evil directed at this created and manipulative idea made an energy that has become tangible. We are creative beings. Our minds are God's mind and as you sow, so shall you reap. It's all there in the Bible, warning us, but we read things in a way that supports our belief system.

Aliens

In the past, scientists have cried away from the possibility of there being life on other planets and UFO sightings were put down to weather balloons, for example. But nowadays there are numerous serious television programmes, books and articles in scientific journals, which speak of there being a strong likelihood that we are not alone in the universe. Of course we're not. Psychics have been saying so for thousands of years and there is a lot of evidence to support it. It is fascinating that the existence of extra-terrestrial life was simply accepted by many ancient tribal civilisations of our world, just as life after death was accepted.

When I was a little girl, my parents, brother and I were driving through Paris. We came to a halt in an enormous traffic jam near the Arc de Triomphe. People were looking up into the sky and pointing, so we got out of the car and looked up too; there was a circular, shiny metal object flitting about in the sky. It moved up and down and from side to side numerous times and then shot straight up in the air so fast that it was gone in a heartbeat. This was reported in the evening paper and then denied a few days later – yes, of course, it was 'a weather balloon'. But hundreds of people saw it that day and it was not a weather balloon. I have actually seen one of those and these two objects were not remotely alike.

When I was in my early teens, I was playing badminton with my brother in the garden. The same type of object appeared out of nowhere, or so it seemed as it arrived so quickly. It hovered about, flitting from side to side just like the one we had seen earlier. It stayed for ages and then suddenly two RAF jets roared overhead and 'buzzed' it; but the UFO was able to stay hovering in one place, so the jets had great difficulty in getting close to it. My father rang the nearest RAF airfield and didn't get much of a reply.

When I was in my late teens, my boyfriend of the time and I stopped in the secluded gateway of the little reservoir at the top of a hill near my family home in Essex, to canoodle (as you do). It was dark and my boyfriend turned off the lights and the engine. We had half an hour before I had to be home. Suddenly the wood to our right was lit up by a bright light emanating from the reservoir. We thought we might be in trouble for parking there and were just considering moving the car... when the next thing we knew was that two hours had passed, the car was cold, as were we, and the light had gone. We were also absolutely terrified, fearful of death – that scared.

We talked for a couple of minutes, realised that we couldn't explain what had happened but knew that something terrible had happened, and then we drove home agreeing that we would never mention it again. From that day onwards for many years, I was unable to talk about that evening or anything to do with aliens; if I saw a picture of a Grey, the little almond-eyed aliens, I would shake uncontrollably and cry. My boyfriend also couldn't speak about it.

Many years later I was persuaded to go to a UFO club meeting. I don't know what made me go but I did, and there was a famous Ufology lecturer there that evening. She talked for a while and I tried to shrink into my chair. I felt sick and I was shaking. She then talked about alien abductions and time loss, turned directly to me and said that I was showing all the classic signs of this. She walked over to me and gave me a sheet of paper and a pencil and, looking deeply into my eyes, told me to draw the thing that took me. Without thinking about it and obeying her instantly, I drew a Grey with webbed fingers. She then opened a portfolio and showed me and the audience loads of identical ones. I felt absolutely driven to destroy my picture, which I did. It was like I was on automatic pilot – this experience freaked me out.

As a teacher within the spiritual movement, I have come across a lot of people with the same kind of experience, but it wasn't until I received healing from a couple who specialise in treating abductees that I was able to help these students. Of course, so many people including Spiritualists (and possibly you?) think that all this is nonsense and that we are making it up. I would have thought so too except that it happened to me. I definitely don't want to remember what was done to me, but it is something that can be treated. There is usually some kind of communication device like a tracker left behind, which cannot be seen with the naked eye, and clearly some sort of hypnosis has been used to engender fear every time the subject comes up.

Well, not all aliens are nasty, of course, just as not all humans are. There are different races of aliens too, those from different planets or those from the same planet but not looking the same. Some aliens are in spirit and are communicating with mediums just like spirit humans do. I had the most amazing experience of teaching a group where one medium was channelling a living telepathic alien and another was being entranced by the spirit of a dead alien – the same race, but one dead and one alive. They were able to converse with one another and spoke in English as they were using the mediums' thoughts to communicate telepathically. They were able to talk about the same things and gave more than enough evidence that they were exactly who they said they were, including good 'overshadowing', like transfiguration, seen by all in the group. Aliens are alive.

So, if you're convinced that I'm nuts, do try not to discard the rest of the book. Keep going!

Nature spirits and Elementals

So now you may be thinking, "What, dead cows, angels and aliens – now she's going on about fairies?" Yes, expand your mind! I've been seeing them since I was six years old and so have most mediums. I also have an 'inspirer' who is the spirit of a tree.

You see, We Are One. There is no difference or disconnection between any living things. It's just a matter of how we are configured: my energy is gathered together to look like Mel while yours is gathered to look like you. There is consciousness in everything because the Great Spirit is everywhere and everything; there is nowhere that the Great Spirit is not, therefore mind is also there. This is the philosophy and knowledge of Shamanism.

I have watched a healer talk to a bush that she is about to prune and seen her ask the bush to withdraw its life force energy from where she is going to cut, so that it doesn't get hurt. The branch literally flopped and the leaves drooped right in front of my eyes. I have talked to a houseplant, asked it to let go of its diseased leaves and it has done so immediately. I have cried against the trunk of an old tree that I have known for many years and the lower branches have stroked my hair. As a medium, I have been entranced by a tree and, incidentally, by a wolf and a dog, and I have become them. They are intelligent and know that we exist. Trees tolerate us as an old man would tolerate a young playful puppy.

One day, I received a 'phone call from a lady and her partner. They were in a state of shock, to say the least. The two ladies had been playing the guitar in their normal, suburban garden and they had lit a fire to keep warm and to bake a couple of spuds, because it's a lovely thing to do. It was a dark evening and the flames built up beautifully. Suddenly, they said, the atmosphere changed and became highly charged with power. The fire went wild and a huge fireball appeared, hovering above the rest of the flames. It then lifted up, floated over to them and hung in the air in front of each of them, one at a time. They said that it was looking at them and they knew that there was a mind there. They said "Hello" and then it returned to the fire, which died back down to normal so they put it out and shot indoors.

I explained that this was the spirit of the fire and that their music had interested it so it wanted to see them more closely. This is why shamans honour and bless the fire. It is a giver of life, security and energy.

One day, I was out with my sons and first husband, walking by a beautiful river. I couldn't walk any further so I sat down on a bench by the river while the menfolk carried on to complete a circuit and find me later. No-one was about, so I went into meditation. I realised that I was being watched, so I opened my eyes and saw a figure completely made of water standing on top of the river and giving me a good hard stare. When it knew that I had seen it, it flowed rapidly across the water and stood as close to me as it could while still attached to the water. It was a water spirit, deeply upset because people had been throwing stuff into the river. I was scared of it because it was very angry indeed. So I explained that I would never do that and promised to encourage people to be more environmentally conscious.

It seems that there is more to life than we realise. I've communicated with all sorts of animals, both living and dead, aliens and things that I don't know how to describe to you. The important thing to realise is that human beings are not the be all and end all of life. This world is not ours to do with as we please. We share it with all sorts of life-forms, as we do the universe.

CHAPTER FIVE

WHAT IS GOD?

I suppose that one way to look at this question is to ask, "What is not God?" and the answer to that is surely quite simple: nothing. There is nothing in the universe that isn't God because God isn't a thing, or a person, or a being. God just is. God doesn't occupy a space but all space, and since that is limitless then God occupies limitlessness. But this implies that God is a being doing that and is 'limitlessness'...

Note that I am avoiding using the word 'He' – or even 'She' – when writing about God, and I'm not going to use 'It' either. What other names could be used for God? Well, Great Spirit is the one that many Spiritualists prefer, usually, frankly, because they have a Native American guide and think that's what the guide would say. It probably is, but the shamanic view of Great Spirit was never like the orthodox Judaeo-Christian view that most of us grew up with. (There are very few born and bred Spiritualists. Most are converts.) Another name we could use, and I am obviously not the first one to coin the expression, is Collective Consciousness or, as I think of it, Higher Self Collective Consciousness. Personally, I tend to use Great Spirit. Yes, I have Native American guides, but it's because it works for me. Let me tell you what I mean.

I never believed that prayer should be that whining sort of "Gimme that please, God, and I'll be a good girl", because this clearly

41

isn't a fair bargain as I am often quite naughty. Still, when I did pray to God I could never understand why, more often than not, the thing I asked for didn't happen, or it happened in another way, or if it did happen as I had asked for, I'd come unstuck. This didn't seem like a loving God who was hearing me and trying to do something to help me. Perhaps some of these thoughts are familiar?

I tried asking the spirit guides to sort things out for me too, thinking like so many Spiritualists do that they were God's messengers. No, still things happened that were extremely unpleasant in my life. I tried the angels and I tried willing things to go my way and for people to do what I wanted, and I definitely fell on my backside when I tried that one. So then I thought, again in the way that many Spiritualists do, that I needed to learn something from the problem, from the pain, and it was a lesson.

I was then left with the thoughts that either God must somehow be vengeful, or that I'd 'agreed' to deal with this awful stuff, or that someone was sending me bad wishes, or that I'd been absolutely horrible in a past life. I had put all my hopes in a separate power that we have been told had created the Earth, and this power would take me home to Him one day and I'd be all better, with no disabilities or pain. We are also told that this Earthly life is about suffering, or so Gautama Buddha said (and so do some Spiritualists). Great! What the hell did we come here for then? We should all have stayed home! So then we're back to the 'here to learn through painful lessons' idea again; somehow this really didn't make sense to me and decades later it still doesn't.

What do I believe or feel I know now? First of all, of course, there is no God meting out punishment: we do suffer, that's true, but much of that is our own doing. I know how hard this life is, believe me, perhaps not as much as a starving orphan in a war-torn country; but I have been sexually and physically abused, beaten, starved, rejected, lied to, and had my life threatened verbally, physically and psychically. I've had ten operations in my life, broken my back, my arms, my ankles and my nose, and I've been cheated on several times romantically and by so-called friends. The list is enormous and this is only the tip of the iceberg. I know all about life's suffering, yet I laugh and smile a lot and I have coped with so much you would not believe. It takes a great deal nowadays for me to cry with sorrow, though I frequently cry with love. I do not see suffering in myself. I see obstacles to climb over, but I refuse to suffer because I see that as being weak.

The point is, you see, I know that I am God. Since God is everywhere, God must be me and not just a spark or a bit of me. If God is omnipresent, there is nowhere that God is not and therefore all of me is also God. So I have the capacity to make things happen if I choose to and, you know, there is no separate being up there in the clouds saying, "Yes, you can have this but not that." Every time we ask God for something or to do something for us, we are giving our power away and effectively saying that we are helpless. No, we are not.

Now of course, Spiritualists know all about personal responsibility: it is roughly the fifth principle of Spiritualism and all the different organisations say something to that effect. It means that we are responsible for everything we do or don't do. Simply put, if we slap someone round the face in a temper it's as if we have slapped ourselves, and no-one can sort out the slapping and ensuing flack afterwards but us. God is not coming down off a cloud to slap us back and neither are the dead people: sometime or other and somehow we shall find a way of slapping ourselves. Nor can we blame the person we slapped for making us do it. No amount of 'Look what you made me do' is going to make good. It was our hand, it's our personal responsibility, we can't pop into a curtained box and ask for forgiveness and twelve Hail Marys will not alter the wrong we have done.

Now, in Spiritualism we don't think as much as we should about how far this goes. We often think about the effects of our actions, but not about why we have personal responsibility. You see, what is the fundamental power that we say God has? Creation. Or another way of looking at it for non-creationists, could be animation – giving life. Have you been present when someone has died? There is a definite leaving, which is why a dead person is often referred to as 'the departed'. The body becomes an empty shell, like an overcoat that's been discarded, and it instantly begins to decay. On the other hand, have you been in a séance room or a development circle when the guides arrive? There is a definite presence, yet there is no body for them to inhabit (unless we're doing deep trance, but that's a whole other subject). In both cases there is a definite awareness of a mind being present, in absence of a body to inhabit. And that's what happens at conception: we begin to inhabit an Earthly form. We animate it. Without this animation, the foetus dies.

Let me explain about ectoplasm here. In the film Ghostbusters, there was a character called Slimer who messed about with ectoplasm and was green. Actually, sometimes ectoplasm is green especially if it is luminous, but it is a substance that can take on any colour and it can also be invisible to the human eye. Spirit teachers, my own and other people's, have explained that this substance is what makes us and it is alterable by the mind. One could think of it as being the structure beneath our bodies, the thing that our forms are created from. This substance is only visible or tangible when it is animated, or thought into, and any mind can think ectoplasm into something. Another name for it is Akasha.[2]

Spirit people animate ectoplasmic forms in the séance room. There is a build-up of ectoplasm and the mind of the spirit person who wishes to communicate animates the form to allow communication that Earthly people can understand. The substance that is used is part

[2] In Hinduism, Akasha is the essence of everything in our world. There are five Hindu elements, similar to the beliefs of Jainism, Buddhism and Shamanism. These five elements are Akasha (also known as ether), earth, water, fire and air.

Akasha's first characteristic is 'sound', referred to in the Bible, the first words of Genesis: "In the beginning was the word and the word was with God." God is said to have created the Earth with the word. In the séance room, sitters are encouraged to speak and to sing. The spirit operators, those responsible for the production of phenomena such as materialisation and IDV (independent direct voice, spirit people speaking for themselves in the room without using the medium's body), tell us that the sound of our voices provides an energy that is used to animate ectoplasm or Akasha.

of the medium and often part of the séance sitters' energy. God doesn't give out an extra bit of life force during the séance, the spirit people borrow it from the Earthly people present with their permission. Please note that very carefully. There is also another energy to be had that is 'free-floating', a sort of kinetic potential power. All this is ectoplasm or Akasha.

These energies give a spirit person from another life dimension the opportunity to communicate with someone here. Mediums don't just use their minds to communicate with spirit. This is very clear in the séance room or when a medium is delivering proof of survival from a public rostrum and stands like the spirit communicator, becomes the communicator's height and build and uses their mannerisms. Mediums are strongly influenced by the thoughts and vibrations of people surrounding them. Mediums use all of themselves to express mediumship and create an image of the communicator to their audience; they use their own physical form, change it and appear as someone else.

Now, that's amazing isn't it? But it happens all the time. Look how we re-create ourselves every single day. A man goes to work, putting on his overalls and picking up his tool bag; he is now a plumber. He looks plumber-like, he can handle a wrench and stop water leaks. Later he comes home to his lovely partner, drops his mates-at-work attitude and becomes a devoted husband, armed with all his love for her. The kids run in exhausted from school and demanding their tea and the same man becomes like a kid himself (or possibly a Victorian). He goes to the pub to watch Arsenal with his mates and he's a team player. Back home to the wife and, as long as he hasn't imbibed too much, he becomes a Lothario and makes love. It's the same man, different selves, probably with a different vocabulary, stance and clothing for each scene of his life. So it is not difficult to see that a medium working properly (if only they were still trained to do that) is doing the same thing, but each persona is actually another mind from the spirit world.

What has this got to do with God? Everything. I am saying that everyone has the power to be whatever they want to be, within the constraints of their geographical location, health and financial situation. These are things you hand-picked anyway because you create your life and your attitude to it. If you choose to be a victim of life's hardships, then you'll be hard up. If you choose to acknowledge the opportunities for learning that there are in all lives, but in a positive and non-suffering way, then you will see yourself for what you really are – a creative and incredibly powerful being.

You are God.

CHAPTER SIX

WHAT AM I?

The last chapter talked about our nature as God. That's all very well on a cosmic level but what about on a day-to-day, mundane level? What are we when horrible things happen or when we are in a rut and nothing changes from one boring day to the next? Are we something else when good things happen? What about those people who seem to have everything their own way, the people who are rich and always successful – are we the same as them?

In an episode of a well-known American cartoon about a dysfunctional family in which we see so much of ourselves, a character said that everyone is good-looking on the inside and that taking part rather than winning is the important thing. Another character says, "Yeah, that's just what ugly failures say." The phrase has been repeated in films and elsewhere too, so it must be something that the general population believes: really, life doesn't seem fair and good-looking people get all the breaks in life, unless of course you know someone (jobs for the boys). So society believes that the shallow things of looks and favours are what get you ahead.

Now, I hate to be cynical here and to join that bandwagon, but once we get out of our hopeful youth – and for some it comes much younger than that – we realise that on a material level the above is one hundred per cent true. One could be the most talented medium in the world but, because you don't fit in with the crowd, you may not have reached the number of people you hoped your offer of service to mankind and Great Spirit would generate. You could tell yourself that this is because you 'needed to learn the lesson of humility' and how to deal with frustration, or you could just face the fact that you just don't know the bigger plan of life from your individualised perspective. Our suffering may have nothing whatsoever to do with our reason for being here, or it may be exactly that: our reason for being here. Our mundane mind doesn't know but our higher mind does.

That seems to be the way to look at life, our place within it and what we are, because the only way we can understand anything is by our relativity. We know that we are small when we look up at Mum, because she's bigger. We know we are female when we recognise other people's shapes, although that doesn't mean we are female on the inside – we discover our sexuality as hormones and thoughts encroach upon us as we grow. We know we are human, or most of us do unless other places are within our current memory, because we are like the others here even if many of us would rather be a butterfly or a puppy from time to time and have their apparent freedom. After all, who wouldn't want to roll about on lovely fresh grass offering our belly for someone kind to rub? Flying without a plane must be cool too.

So, we observe life from where we think we are, from where we perceive ourselves to be. Yet we are capable of empathising with other creatures and we can take ourselves off into our imagination, into visualisation, into a daydream, a book or a film, into space or another time… We are actually limitless, mentally and spiritually – that's part of the illusion of individuality and the we-are-God thing.

So what happens when we use that limitless wandering mind and spirit to investigate what we really are? Well, then we find visions, feelings and experiences that don't fit in with what society and our education tell us. Eventually these experiences will be backed up by science, just like the discoveries that the Earth isn't flat and that the brain is not the mind (a recent discovery that scientists are still arguing about because many are terrified of being ridiculed for their investigations and subsequent beliefs). And if we accept what we see, feel and experience in our mental wanderings, if we have a trusting and true relationship with our spirit guides, if we allow inspiration to flow to us from the higher realms of consciousness, then we start to make sense of how life works and realise that we really aren't just this bag of bones.

You know, it all boils down to that: we are not just this bag of bones. This life is just a phase, a period in our existence when we experience limitation. It's an experiencing place, a sounding board, feeling what suffering is in this particular way, feeling what joyfulness is in this particular way. It's really important though. It's not Hell, although it can feel like it; it's also not Heaven, although it can feel like that too. It's just a dimension of life to have a go at and it's perfectly natural for us to do it. That's all there is to it.

So what is this 'higher mind'? We've talked about being the observer in life, that sometimes it can feel like we are outside ourselves and looking at life as if someone else were living it. We've also established that the person we think we are, here on Earth, is just a fragment of what we really are and that this incarnation of ours is an illusion. I would like to quote the Buddha here:

"Do not live in the world, in distraction and false dreams, outside the dharma.[3]

Arise and watch. Follow the way joyfully through this world and beyond.

Follow the way of virtue. Follow the way joyfully through this world and on beyond!

For consider the world – a bubble, a mirage. See the world as it is and death shall overlook you.

---

[3] The dharma is eternal law, which is in everything.

Come, consider the world, a painted chariot for kings, a trap for fools. But he who sees goes free.

As the moon slips from behind a cloud and shines, so the master comes out from behind his ignorance and shines.

The world is in darkness. How few have eyes to see! How few the birds who escape the net and fly to Heaven!

Swans rise and fly toward the sun. What magic! So do the pure conquer the armies of illusion and rise and fly.

If you scoff at Heaven and violate the dharma, if your words are lies, where will your mischief end?

The fool laughs at generosity. The miser cannot enter Heaven. But the master finds joy in giving and happiness is his reward.

And more – for greater than all the joys of Heaven and Earth, greater still than dominion over all the worlds, is the joy of reaching the stream."

–FROM THE DHAMMAPADA

The reason I have included this quotation here is two-fold. First, I have found Buddhist philosophy to be extremely helpful in my efforts to understand myself and I would like to suggest that those interested in understanding themselves more would benefit from reading Buddhist literature. Secondly, this one quotation speaks volumes all by itself. It refers to living within the natural law of the universe, thus ending karma and rebirth and kind living, to mention just a few things.

This quotation highlights exactly what we are, creatures seeking one answer to the question "How can I be happy?" If we cut to the chase, isn't that all we want? We may want a variety of things, like a partner, a nice home, a television, money, a bigger car, kids… the list of wanting is so long. But we want these things because we think they will make us happy and this if of course the suffering that Buddha talks of. One man's suffering may be another man's joy. Again, we are back to relativity. But the bottom line is "I want to be happy."

Have you found that the more you work on yourself and mature spiritually, the fewer things you want? Have you found that the more you give of yourself in a selfless and unconditionally loving way, the more joyful you feel? Most of us have been taught that things don't make us happy although, as I have mentioned before, it's not so easy to be happy when we have nothing and are starving or, worse still, when we see people we love starving. It seems easier to be giving when we have spare to give, but the most valuable thing we have to give is actually our time. Even though time only exists in a world of endings and beginnings, and in this life it is something that we have a limited amount of, nevertheless even if we have no money to give others we do have time. It is therefore precious and perhaps we need to find more ways in which to share it with others.

Now, the higher mind is that part of us that is observing our life being lived. It is not affected by time passing at all. It is always 'in the stream', the flow, and has full awareness of the whole of life. We are aware of it when we know right from wrong because this part of us knows exactly what should or shouldn't be done; it is our conscience, in a sense, but it is more than that. This part of us isn't mean, angry or despondent. It doesn't have emotion but is unconditional love. Simply put, this part of us is always in God and is transcendent.

So, what are we? We are human beings, which means that we are spiritual in nature and incarnate into bodies as required for the planet we have chosen to live on. Our spirit is eternal but our bodies are not. Although our higher mind knows everything, we don't when we are within the body and this is natural and deliberate. Our natural calling is to be at one with all life, because that is our natural state, but our goal is to attain that while unaware. This strengthens the power of the whole, so in effect all that is, or God, or Great Spirit, is always growing and changing, which is the natural state of all life. Nothing is static, everything is reacting and moving. Life is change and that is the case on all levels of life. A phrase White Owl often uses is, 'Perfection is always more perfect!' So we must not think that our journey is ever going to end because it can't – that's how life is. The striving for an end to suffering, and the experience of being cut off from the whole, are what drive humanity forward.

We might like to think of ourselves as 'change'. One of the easiest ways to feel happier is to accept this change and to find contentment in the present moment, not waiting for the perfect life to arrive so we can then be happy in it. Even if perfection seemed to come into our lives, we would still find discontentment. What am I? I am an eternally existing, limitless, formless yet formable if required, vibrational, multi-dimensional life-form. This is my natural state.

CHAPTER SEVEN

ENLIGHTENMENT

Many of us think that enlightenment means 'knowing everything' and we assume that it happens all at once. But that isn't it. Enlightenment tends to come as flashes of insight that strike us, sometimes shockingly and causing a sharp intake of breath, that 'light bulb moment' – and then the hard work comes as we try to make sense of what we have suddenly come to know along with all the other truths that we hold within. The really difficult part comes when we can't make the older things we thought we knew fit in with this fresh knowing.

When the Buddha reached enlightenment whilst sitting under the Bodhi tree, he had to organise himself too. He came from a wealthy and powerful family and had to live his life completely differently in order to bring what he knew into line with how he wanted to live. We all do this too when we discover something new; we change our lifestyles and sometimes these enlightened changes are a challenge for our loved ones around us.

In the Bible, it is said that Jesus told his twelve disciples that they would have to leave their families and everything behind and follow him. They did so. So convincing and overwhelming was the truth they found with Jesus that they just upped and went. They became wandering preachers and, just like many Spiritualists, they left one faith for another. I imagine that the disciples' families must have thought that their sons had gone mad and had been drawn into some evil cult or other. How similar is this to many Spiritualists' journeys?

But when a truth hits us between the eyes in an enlightening moment, there is no going back from it. It's not like a little thought that we can take or leave. It's a conviction, an inner knowing that surges through our being and there's no getting away from it. For me, the start of enlightenment (and I've not finished yet) was during a simple shared meditation.

I was sitting in meditation, in a row, in a Spiritualist venue with around two hundred other people. The venue in question was not one that had brought me any peace whatsoever as the people who were apparently teaching me were incredibly cruel and not remotely spiritual. I had heard them saying the most dreadful things about other students. My reason for being there was to finish off a qualification and I intended to acquire this because I thought I needed it so as to be free to work and teach within most Spiritualist environments. I have in fact discarded this qualification since then along with the other ones I obtained from this organisation, realising that the only qualification I needed was to offer myself in service to God. Instead I chose to become ordained as a Spiritualist minister within a much more broadly loving organisation and I am driven to support fellow workers for God in a manner that is nurturing and loving.

When I had completed my meditation and the experience that I shall describe had occurred, the teachers who had formed the meditation group, rather than being kind and supportive accused me of lying and of making up what I had said. I told them what had happened because I was overwhelmed by love. Please note, then, that the environment you find yourself in has not one jot of influence on what happens within your soul, unless of course you think it will.

Here's what happened. The psychic power in the room was incredible. This was caused by the number of people present and the fact that most of them were nice and that the room had been used for decades for spiritual work. So, even though the people running things were dark, the souls who came from the spiritual realms were filled with light most of the time. I felt myself being approached by a very strong but incredibly kind energy. It was a spirit guide, someone whom I knew very well although he had never approached me in this particular way. I realised that I was held within a love that was pure and safe. This was why I was unaffected by the hostility towards me in the room from the living.

Suddenly, I was lifted out of my body and straight up through the top of my head. I shot up in the air and passed through the roof of the building and into the sky, soaring upwards still and through a kind of barrier that was around the Earth. It looked like the Earth's horizon and I was in space. I continued upwards, passing stars and planets and what looked like clouds, and as I travelled onwards I realised that my body had gone and had been replaced by a silver one. My features had gone too and sometimes I was outside looking back at myself; I looked soft around the edges as if I had none. Sometimes I was inside where my body ought to have been. I found myself within an enormous expanse of light; in fact, I couldn't see where the light began or where it ended.

Then the love came.

I was engulfed by a love that was total, complete, sweeping through every part of me. For what could have been seconds or a whole lifetime, I became absolutely everyone and everything. I was vast and tiny. I was significant and insignificant. I knew everything. I knew what was going to happen for the whole universe. I saw destruction and creation. I was. And at that moment, I knew that I was safe and that absolutely everything that has happened in the world and is happening now and will happen, was exactly as it is meant to be. The love was one huge being that I was also.

Then I felt myself being gently let go of, though with a feeling of reassurance that this was okay too. I cried when the love first hit me and then I cried again as I lost my awareness of it. It never really let me go, I know that too, but I just couldn't live here and also be aware of it to that extreme. I couldn't function as a human being. I would have been formless and away from here. Dead, I guess, but beyond the spirit world. I knew too that not everyone was conscious of this love and wholeness. Spirit people were not there either. This was about a level of understanding and one that we can't hold in this dimension. It is as far removed from human individualised illusion as you can get, a complete at-one-ment, something feared by people who want to be 'a person'.

As a child, I'd had moments of awareness that there were dimensions of life outside human experience, when I met fairies and communicated with trees and animals. But amazing as these experiences were, this first connection to God, this moment of enlightenment, changed me forever. It is something that can't fully be explained to others. They have to have it for themselves and this is what I have now dedicated my life to. I am not remotely interested in mediumship development, although I will do my best to help you to be as good as you can be at it if that's what you need on your journey to enlightenment. I am more interested in your kindness and gentleness to others. I would like you to feel this love.

I have had many other moments of sitting within this incredible love and it is not the same as 'sitting in the power', a method taught for enhancing psychic energy for mediumistic work. No, this is about the Divine, which is not mediumship, although absolutely any work in the world can be divine. One can sweep the road with God. One can be an instrument to heal the sick with God and one can be a heavenly psychic. But one can also be a bastard while sweeping the road, one can gorge oneself on praise while being an instrument to heal the sick and, yes, healing energy will still get through. And who hasn't come across the lost psychics and mediums, guided by something other than they think they are?

Now, I am not enlightened. Like many others, I believe that I should be 'without sin' if I am enlightened. I do try hard but hey, I eat too much, don't exercise enough and swear from time to time (my friends carry a swear box when I'm part of a Q&A panel). I have had moments of enlightenment and there are things I do that I am proud of, which in itself is probably not a good thing. I will not deliberately hurt anyone and I beat myself up if a moth crashes into my windscreen when I drive my very environmentally clean car. But I still have a car.

Society dictates what good behaviour is and I don't think I'll get time off for it. Anyway, the only person who can tell me what being good is, is me. I have that still small voice within me that tells me off, just as everyone has. Our conscience is our guide, that's true. The tough thing is actually listening to it, or developing the ability to hear it in the first place. The things I am telling you in this book are the things that have come to me over the years as a result of my moments of enlightenment. I know that I chose to come back to the Earth. Idiot! Whether this denotes enlightenment, I don't know. It's a kind of oxymoron – what enlightened being would be foolish enough to come back here?

Although we need to have experiences, good and bad, in order to grow, we are not sent here by some separate force and nor are we here alone. You will see that I write a great deal about how We Are One and it is important to understand what that means on so many levels. Quite simply, the experiences that I have been describing have proved to me that I am not separate from anything, from anyone, anywhere or any time. It doesn't even matter if someone is dead; just because they are no longer in my dimension doesn't mean that they don't exist anymore. My work and the work of mediums throughout time has shown that.

This lack of separation talks to me of omnipresence and, without any desire to appear grandiose or arrogant, this tells me that we are divine, eternal and able to create. The force that animates trees, people, water, air and everything else is within us and we can all manifest things. We are conduits for this animating energy and our soul is divine. We don't 'fall' to Earth, we steer to Earth. The degree of awareness we have of such incarnation is irrelevant but the uncovering of awareness starts a whole new ball game. Once we know, then we must accept responsibility for our actions, thoughts, inactions and lack of consideration. We are attracted quite naturally to the life and the body that we need to become fully enlightened. This attraction is quite natural and normal. It is exactly how things operate in our world – electron to electron.

We also attract someone to walk with us and I have mentioned these beings a lot too. Spirit guides are people, animals or devic beings who are drawn to us, sometimes from before conception in our mothers' wombs, right throughout our lives. Some come and go, as specialists, and some don't leave; our main guide, also known as a doorkeeper or gatekeeper, doesn't leave until after our death and then for as long as we need them. These beings are with us to help us reach enlightenment and to carry out the experiences we have been drawn to and to learn from them. This may be with full consciousness of our guides, if we have some awareness, or more usually it is with very little awareness at all. Most people feel they have some purpose, but most don't know what that is.

On this path to enlightenment, we have help. That's good, isn't it?

CHAPTER EIGHT

WHY SOME PEOPLE
ARE CRUEL

Why are some people cruel? When will our world stop crying and begin to mend? Will those people who take advantage of others in the name of religion become accountable for their actions?

These are three questions that I have often been asked. I think that everyone with a heart will have asked the first question many times in their lives; those without won't have asked it and they are probably the ones being cruel. It seems that some people just don't see other people, animals or nature as being of any significance and are truly selfish. They don't care about anyone other than themselves, so they show no respect or consideration to others. There are others who don't know how to show love to anyone or anything, including themselves, and are cruel to themselves too. Perhaps we would describe these people as being mentally ill.

There are those who see other people as obstacles between themselves and their goals, which are usually power- or money-based goals. Of course, those who follow a spiritual path will say that material things don't lead to happiness; but life does feel a lot more pleasant when one has a roof over one's head and food on the table. The important thing to remember is balance: we need enough but not so much that we become more afraid of losing what we have, whether that be power or possessions.

I think we can agree that making someone cry or jump back in shock or scream in terror or pain, and that killing, maiming or causing deliberate harm, are all terrible things and are wrong. If we do any of these things, they will come back to bite us either through society's punishment or through spiritual amends. Literally, we get back as we give out, and I have seen that the closer a person is to reaching moments of enlightenment in their life then the quicker that biting will be. Sometimes we bring something back to ourselves almost immediately; we might say something hurtful and wham, something unpleasant happens to remind us of how nasty we've just been. Those who are more blind to their spiritual nature seem to take longer, in Earthly terms, to get bitten. We often ask, "Why do the baddies get away with it?" Well, often it is so because their blindness is so powerful that the nudging of karma doesn't reach through their thick skin. Of course, there are forces much bigger than karmic nudging and I can think of numerous disgustingly behaved people who have been booted very severely by the energy of their misdeeds catching up with them.

Some two decades ago, I held a circle in my little cottage. It was one of those where the bathroom and toilet were downstairs, which becomes relevant later in the story. Two of my circle members were very close friends, lived near each other and spent a great deal of time together. I began to notice that they had become a little distant from one another and I then received a 'phone call from one of them saying that she was really worried about her friend. She was apparently spending a great deal of time with "a group of spiritual people" in their local town; she had been told that she had to wear her head covered at all times 'to protect her chakras' and must spend most of her time in the home of this group's leader. This was also troubling for the lady's husband; they had young kids and she was leaving her kids unattended so that their Dad had to try and look after them. He couldn't get through to his wife and she seemed to be drugged.

Both ladies had stopped coming to the circle because the one who was behaving oddly was the driver. The lady on the `phone had asked her friend if she could visit this other group, but she was frightened to go alone so we went together.

We entered a very dark and gloomy mid-terrace house. There was a smell like incense though it was possibly cannabis or something like that. The man in charge was from Haiti. When I had sat down he gave me a drink of water, which I noticed he handled with great care, not touching anywhere near the top of the glass, so I knew immediately not to drink it or even touch the glass. I told him that I was there about this lady and that I was concerned for her. He told me in a hypnotic voice that I was not to worry about her and then made a peculiar movement with his hand towards me; I saw how the movement directed energy at me and I fended it off with a gentle flick of my own hand. It then became like something out of The Lord of the Rings, with Gandalf fighting Saruman. After a while, the man laughed and said that I was a very powerful psychic and that I should leave. We had barely spoken.

After we left, I spent a short while dealing with a psychic attack from this man. The smell from his house permeated mine for a couple of hours until I banished him.

I awoke needing a trip downstairs and there in the middle of the kitchen was the lady we'd been concerned about, in astral form. This means that she was out of her body and was using the first layer of her auric field, her astral body, to walk around in. She cried out for help and then vanished, so I sent healing. This went on for two weeks and she woke me several times a night, but when I tried to telephone her there was never an answer. I also tried to visit her but she was never home.

Then one night, I was very tired and she was there again. I lost my patience and temper, told her to "Sod off!" and stumbled back to bed. The following morning the `phone rang and it was her. All she said was, "No, you sod off!" I was amazed! She was conscious of leaving her body and was genuinely calling out for help, but couldn't do so while in her body. I had never come across this kind of horrible outside influence from someone before and didn't know what to do, but my guides did. I spoke with a witch who works with me from time to time. At this point in my life, I was a bit wary of her but I figured that if anyone knew what to do then Esmerelda would. Boy, did she. I sat with her, 'off we went' and all I know is that we fought something that was holding onto the woman.

A couple of days later her friend rang me to say that the woman had gone to see her, had uncovered her hair and said that she didn't want to go to the Voodoo priest's house anymore. I had guessed that this was his path, but it was a dark path of Voodoo. I have met other people since who follow that way and they are most definitely not horrible people. Like any path in life, it is our intention and what we use energy for that determines whether our actions are evil or good. Well, a month later the priest's house burned to the ground, killing his two sons. The fire was started by candles used in the building. He was apparently a broken man. I will leave you to draw your own horrible conclusions, as I did.

The cruellest person I have ever known was my mother. She is long in the spirit world and is not the same as she was when on Earth. I wouldn't describe her improvement as being learning, more of a remembering or unfolding. I have distinct memories of my existence before incarnation and I know that I chose to be her scapegoat, the one she would still be able to get her hands on and vent her vicious words on. Indeed, my sister was taken away at birth and put up for adoption (I would dearly love to find her) while my brother was put into Care as a small boy; my father did not even know that Mum had previously been married or that she had a son at all. But I was left with her as we moved abroad.

Although I am messed up in many ways because of her behaviour towards me, I know that it was not personal. I can say that on many levels. On an Earthly level, it was not personal because she was seriously mentally ill and had often been an in-patient in a mental institution from childhood, therefore not accountable for her behaviour. On a spiritual level, we are not individuals at all and life everywhere, in whatever dimension and on whatever plane, is about experience and attempting to live collectively with love and compassion despite being under the illusion of individuality. I am not distinct from anyone else, therefore all that I do and don't do is for me and for others because We Are One.

Nothing in life is really personal. We think that we are being aimed at. We think that people are taking over land and blowing others up because we are equipped with an instinct for survival and procreation, as are all animals. But if we look at it all from a spiritual perspective, we see that it is not someone else on the other side of the planet blowing up strangers – this is just how it appears when we are living in a relatively safe and prosperous country like the UK, compared to the abject poverty and life struggle of, say, Syria – but it is we who are blowing ourselves up. With that realisation, as We Are One, doesn't it all seem rather ridiculous?

That doesn't prevent us from feeling horrified and disgusted, of course, and it certainly should not prevent us from stopping despots ruling or preventing people from being indoctrinated into terrorist activities. Nor should that knowledge stop us trying to cure cancer or asthma. We must work towards a happy, healthy and peaceful world; and we must include an element of spiritual guidance within that, not just practical help, or how will people realise that fighting and suffering is a poor choice? When I say 'spiritual guidance', I don't mean religious guidance – these are two different things.

So why are people cruel? It is because they are under that impression that they are separate from others and probably there is a little bit of fear in there too, so that they have to be harsh to get what they want. They believe that fulfilling that wanting will make them happy. No, it won't. Accountability – do we get our just desserts? Yes, but not necessarily in the way we expect. I may be suffering in this life for something that I did many hundreds of years ago when I was a Celt, but most of my suffering is because I chose to allow my mother and soul group the opportunity to learn about mental illness through my being the victim. I am no longer the victim and I use my experience to help others.

And when will the world stop crying?
When everyone realises that the sorrow one person feels
is their own too.

CHAPTER NINE

PROBABILITY AND SYNCHRONICITY

I once took part in an experiment measuring the number of times a psychic could 'guess' the colour of a card when it was only seen by the person holding the cards. The tester would hold up cards one after another so that the back of the card faced the psychic and he or she couldn't see the front. There were no reflective surfaces around, the psychic didn't know the tester and the test was carried out several times with different testers. By the laws of probability, the psychic should have got half of them right if they were simply guessing. The more times this is carried out, the chances of correct colours being stated remains the same; but there is some random variation involved and the testers said that any result between three and seven correct guesses out of ten on average would be normal according to 'chance'. Any higher score than that would be 'significant'.

Now, I'm usually rubbish at this sort of thing. My brother would get ten out of ten, which freaked me out, and the pressure to perform has always been an issue with me. When I started, I got eight out of ten. But then I made the mistake of looking at the tester who pulled a face, which I took to mean that I was doing badly when in fact I was getting them all right. The doubt I felt affected my work and from then on I was always 'seeing' the colours two cards ahead of the tester – for example, my first choice would match the tester's third card and so on, right through to the end of the test. So of course my last two choices were incorrect – or were they? I still wonder if I'd picked the first two colours of the next test that someone else would take.

The point of this story is that the laws of probability were challenged that day as over half of the psychics tested did better than the expected average. One person got all their choices right every time, which startled the investigators. They did a lot of mumbling that day. This leads me to think of something that Lana, one of my inspirers, refers to as 'critical mass'. This concept means that when a sufficient number of people do something then it becomes a learned behaviour when previously it was not. She states often that, as We Are One, if enough individualised spirits here on Earth carry out something then everyone else will soon do it too. It is the power of the many overcoming the actions of the few; but, she says, it is not the quantity of people or individualised spirits that matters but the energy and the intention behind the actions and where that comes from. If an intention is from unconditional love and there is enough purity of spirit, then numbers are less relevant. This is why she encourages people to look at their motivations in life and also at their meditation practice; if there are enough people in a space and spiritual work is encouraged, then the power becomes accentuated and can be used. Hence the power of group healing and meditation, the power contained within a church, temple or synagogue, or indeed in a cabinet used for physical mediumship. The manner in which one sits also has a bearing. Sitting in a circle is the most natural of shapes in our world for example, and if we sit with body language that says, "I'm not joining in!" then the power available is dispersed. Harmony in any work in the world is vital. A happy office or factory is a productive one.

I have lost count of how many times I have shocked someone by giving them information that I can't know, as I am sure many of you have. I have lost count of the number of times a parking space has miraculously turned out to be exactly where I visualised it. Many mediums dwell on the one message in the hundreds they give that the recipient hasn't been able to place, and forget about the many that have been happily accepted. We get it right far more often than wrong in our work as mediums – as long as we are motivated and guided correctly, I might add. And surely, if our work is not genuine, as the sceptics would have everyone believe, then we seem to defy probability and averages.

It is annoying when people make generalisations but have clearly never been to see a good medium! I don't try to persuade them anymore as they are too closed-minded, but occasionally a little something will be said and they look suitably stunned (then of course they find an excuse). Two such moments stand out for me.

I was again taking part in an investigation into mediumship, this time with scientists from a university in America. A colleague of theirs had passed over and they wanted to know if he could communicate. He did, through me particularly, and one of the scientists was convinced while the other thought that I had read up on the man. This would have been very clever because I didn't even know his name except that it was John, and then only because John in spirit told me. John was furious that his colleague wouldn't listen, even though this was the experiment they had agreed upon for whichever of them passed over first; his colleagues followed their agreement to do the analysis but then refused to accept the resulting communication. Scream! I can still remember John's deep frustration. He kept bursting into my mind and I would say something to his colleagues like, "There are no aliens here!"; in this particular instance the colleague asked me why I had said that and I told him that I felt inspired to. The one scientist just responded that I was very clever to find out that this was one of John's sayings. Poor man. I can feel him here as I type. "Boy, are they going to feel dumb when they pass over!" he just said.

One day I was watching a daily quiz show that I particularly enjoy, which involves getting the lowest score possible. The studious presenter gave out the answers, which included the word 'apport', explaining that this is an object that appears from nowhere in a séance room. He then added that this never happens. I was furious. How does he know? Has he ever been in a séance room? Has he ever experienced the arrival of an apport or witnessed an asport (when something is taken away)? Grrr, I thought he was more intelligent than that. Well, as John says, "Boy, is he going to feel dumb…"

So is science such a good thing? Of course it is. Without it we wouldn't understand so much of our universe and a lot more of us would die horribly; but there is more to find and know, much more, and gradually science is uncovering what mysticism has always known. When I have talked about synchronistic occurrences to sceptics they have said that it's just luck or coincidence. But when the coincidence becomes ridiculously obvious, then they just have to accept that it isn't a coincidence!

I once asked a friend of mine to draw a medicine card; these are large cards in a pack that have a different animal pictured on each one, and the book that accompanies them describes the qualities or 'medicine' that the animal offers. They can give an insight into life's dilemmas. My friend drew 'hummingbird' and we read the meaning. It was something a little challenging and, being the partial sceptic that she is, my friend said that the card drawn is a matter of luck and she wasn't going to do anything based on just drawing a card. This is of course very sensible, particularly if you are not used to working inspirationally and don't recognise the energy of that. So I shuffled the cards thoroughly and she drew again; she drew that same card five times before giving up and accepting its meaning. This was not coincidence and certainly not luck (and yes, they were well shuffled, not marked, and she even closed her eyes).

White Owl, my teaching guide and trance control (which means that he organises what happens when I'm in an altered state of consciousness), explains that when we realise that We Are One with all life, then there is nothing that we cannot affect with our thought. He is a shaman, although he would never say so, and he has sent owls (real living flying ones) to me, to other members of my soul group and to my students, literally hundreds of times. My students dream about owls, found that they had lots of owl things like ornaments at home, have them fly by extremely closely in the day and at night, fly and stop and stare at them, have three to five different ones appear by them in one day when they were in trouble… you name it, he brings owls. Let me share some of my experiences with you.

I was sitting on a garden lounger while meditating and another of my guides, a Tibetan lama, appeared hovering in mid-air (as they do) right in front of me. I had opened my eyes suddenly for no apparent reason while in a deep altered state of consciousness and there he was. Frankly, I don't know if he materialised or if I was seeing him subjectively. But boy, was he vivid. He looked intently at me, and sent his thoughts to me for some time. The long and the short of it was that if I could just focus on my breath for one hour and have no other thoughts other than breathing in and breathing out, then he would teach me. Pop, then he was gone.

So I used a timer, set it for an hour and sat observing my breath. Several times I got to exactly fifty-nine minutes and thought "Whoopee! I've done it!" then felt his gentle presence and knew that I had failed. There was no recrimination, just understanding. I carried on practising for two years and eventually I made it. He came into my mind and gently said, "Well done. Now you know what I wanted to teach you." I burst out laughing and went indoors.

I sat outside there under a brolly in all weathers as it felt better to sit peacefully with the sounds of nature. The next day I again sat outside, wondering what I would do now that my task of the past two years was done. Again I opened my eyes for no apparent reason and watched as a beautiful white barn owl flew down the side of my house, along a very narrow pathway with only just enough room for its wingspan. It flew straight at me and touched my cheek as it passed, then flew through the arch behind me and away. This was in broad daylight. The touch was solid and I felt the quills really strongly. I took this experience to be the encouragement it was meant as.

Some years later, after a particularly difficult part of my life, I heard a bang from the kitchen. Something had hit the window. There was the perfect imprint of a white bird on the glass. I left it there for some time until we sold the house.

I always have an owl present itself to me in the evening of a service day. Either the owl will be sitting right by the road as I go by, or it will sit in the middle of the road to make me stop (there's never another car about), or fly by my side (this is an experience several of my close friends and soul group members have had), or hoot and screech at my bedroom window until I acknowledge it. I get given owl things and one of the pieces of art I did for my A Level was an ink drawing of an owl. The list is endless and the synchronicity of special owl things is perfect. White Owl always sends an owl when I am distressed and in a particularly splendid way.

Probably the most wonderful owl thing that he has done, though, is actually to materialise his own lower arm and hand alongside my own so that he could physically hold my hand as I grieved for the loss of my first husband. Isn't that spectacular? I don't know if I cried more before or after he did it. No, my first husband didn't die, he just preferred other women to me; but, let me tell you, the grief was enormous. This may sound dreadful to some, but try to understand it from a medium's perspective: if he had died, I would still be able to see him and speak to him. I do know how it feels to be bereaved and I am not being insensitive to those who are widowed – in my job and with my life that would be impossible. But to those whose love has been unrequited, I also know how you feel.

So if you have a series of weird and inexplicable happenings that defy coincidence and remind you of a particular loved one who has passed to spirit, please accept the love. It is not easy for someone who is in another dimension to touch us here. Their love is undying.

CHAPTER TEN

MEDIUMSHIP AND PSYCHISM

Is communicating with the spirit world easy? Is it simple or do we overcomplicate it? On one level, inter-dimensional communication is simple in that it is natural and we do it a lot without realising it. On another level, it is not something that we can do easily if under pressure. One of the severest pressures is when mediums and psychics are asked to 'perform' and to produce phenomena over and over again in a repetitive manner. This is usually when paranormal researchers are observing or when scientists want mediums to carry out an experiment repeatedly to check for things like randomness. Scientists who are closed-minded tend to put all that people like me do down to coincidence. Of course, they also check for fraud and there are undoubtedly lots of fraudulent mediums and psychics about, just as there are in other walks of life; but surely we've proved life after death enough?

So what is mediumship and how does it work? From the years of observation that I have had as a teacher in this field, I believe that mediumship – in a Spiritualist sense, communicating with spirit people – is a completely natural part of being human, like sneezing and smiling. It is not something paranormal. It is normal. But just as some people are

Mozarts, others can only manage to play a tune with one finger. There are different levels of ability and different ways in which we do things.

Some talk about brainwave synchronisation and alterations to brain chemistry, but basically we have an innate function that allows us to communicate mentally with all life. Yes, all life – it isn't just something to talk to dead people with. We use the same telepathic faculties to communicate with the living; some people can totally read other's thoughts while some only get an inkling. Pet owners (or is that co-habitants?) tell us that their pets understand what they are saying and that they know what their dog or cat needs. In recent studies, zoologists have discovered that certain animals have some comprehension of words. I hope that one day soon they will prove what animal lovers already know, that all animals are sentient.

There are also forms of life that are invisible to the human eye but nonetheless exist. Not all of these are truly invisible, they are just microscopic, while some are invisible because they are outside our range of vision although animals can see them, and others are just slightly out of harmony with us, as if they are out of phase. I am talking about nature spirits, angels, devas and beings like that. Sometimes we have just a sense of their presence but nevertheless we are aware of them at some level.

Mediums and psychics are more aware of these than 'normal' people (ah, who would wish to be called 'normal'?). Just as birds use the magnetic field of the Earth to navigate, we are aware of influences within our auric field. I liken it to a spider being aware of a fly caught in its web; we are aware of the vibration that occurs in our aura when someone approaches, whether that is a spirit being or someone still wearing a body. We also 'know' a great deal about that approaching someone within a nanosecond. Our bodies react to the approach – we call that clairsentience – but many mediums have been trained not to notice that so much and only to notice the words and thoughts that come into their minds. This ignores the fact that our whole physical mechanism is in communication with the approaching vibration.

People make us feel. We know instantly when we dislike someone or something. We are taught not to take things and people at face value and to give the benefit of the doubt; but our first impression is usually right and this applies to how we pick up on spirit people and how we pick up on each other if we are working on a psychic level, not specifically tuned into spirit. How often have you felt ill standing next to someone? It is often not that they are draining your energy or sending you 'bad vibrations', rather that they don't feel well and we are picking up that information from them. They are not sending the information to us, we just naturally communicate with one another, because of course We Are One. So the communication is instantaneous, just like a pain in the body talking to the nerves to tell the brain that there is a problem, and the mind knowing this. It's the same process even though it looks like it is coming from someone else.

If we take that on board, we realise that we are actually communicating mediumistically and psychically all the time… yes, all the time. When we 'tune in' to work with clairvoyance, for example, we are just noticing the communication – the information transference. It's our intention behind the desire to receive information that affects our ability to be aware of it. We are actually perfectly capable of knowing absolutely everything all the time, but that's a scary thing and potentially a hazard. I have had moments of that and it has actually been amazing and filled with love; but I would find it difficult to live my material life with that going on all the time. Instead, I choose when I would like to have that level of awareness, in meditation.

So actually mediumship and using psychic gifts are both easy things to do. The hard part is tuning into the bit you want to focus on and understanding what you receive. While being conscious of our individuality yet receiving everything all the time, it is hard to know which bit is coming from where. Indeed, one of the dangers of mediumship development is being overwhelmed with a sense of enormity of it all and believing that we are as powerful as the whole, or God if you like. Whereas we are that, of course, we are not while we are here; if we try to use that power for ourselves, this is what we call 'evil' and that power will come back to bite us! Motivation and intention are the keys here.

I wonder if what mediums do will ever be seen as usual, common and natural. Perhaps not, as long as there are those who like to use the gifts as power-generating tools. It will probably take science to convince people that We Are One. I would like to feel that I could just tell people what I do when they ask me, but often I daren't because people are so bigoted sometimes. It is really important to understand the complete normality of mediumship and psychism when travelling a path of spiritual development. If we get on our high horse about it and think we're special, then we run the risk of losing sight of the point of it: we are here to help those who don't know how to communicate clearly.

The more we work on enlightenment, the wider the content of the messages we give. I remember that as a younger woman I was absolutely determined to blow people away with evidence of survival. Although, yes, it is important to make an audience or congregation jump with shock at one's accuracy, this is to awaken the minds of those who don't know and has nothing whatsoever to do with spirituality. It's all about the needs of the audience and congregation, and the spirit guides know what is needed. So if evidence is needed, and you're attuned to the needs of the many rather than to your own, that's what you'll give. If they need something else, that's what you'll give instead.

And if a medium gets high on the approbation and applause they receive, they need to get over themselves and realise that this doesn't mean they're on the right path. There is a difference between cold, hard evidence and warm, hard evidence. A medium should try to deliver the love that comes from someone's deceased loved one within their message, relaying it with emotion sent through the heart and in the words used. Then if the recipient and perhaps the other people in the room too are touched by this love, then this is heartfelt work and the medium can feel good about it because they have been honest and have delivered the message with excitement for the good it will do. Good loving mediumship is a true by-product of spiritual enlightenment.

Just doing what comes naturally is nothing special. It's how we work with it that matters.

Some people are afraid of following a spiritual path, the realisation that they may have to modify their lifestyle being scary. In Spiritualism, for example, it is said that this is a way of life and so there will be things that we need to change about ourselves. But there is no strict creed, dress code or way of eating. Spiritualists expect each other to be kind and to follow the principles; these vary slightly from one organisation to another but basically say that We Are One, that we believe in God, that there is life after death and that if we behave badly there are consequences and if we behave kindly there are others, but much more pleasant. Life is clearly not that simple, though.

In all walks of life, some people are horrible and use their position in life to boss others about and to be generally unpleasant. That is also certainly true in religion and on the spiritual path. A fear that some developing mediums and psychics talk about is that of becoming 'super sensitive' and having to deal with unpleasant people and situations. As a medium, yes, you are likely to come across bereaved people with loved ones who have passed away in dreadful circumstances, and it's not nice when you see that. Also, people come to you because you are the last resort: they might have terminal illnesses or other awful things going on in their lives such as paedophilia, rape, violence, homelessness and debt; they don't know where else to go and a medium is the only thing left to try.

So this path can be frightening from the perspective of what you may experience in an Earthly sense, and of course it can be frightening from a spooky perspective. There is so much misinformation in the media about ghosts and hauntings that some people believe vampires and the spinning-head-possessed are real. There are indeed restless spirits, possessions and hauntings, but if one understands what the spirit world is and how energy can be stored in buildings and places, then the fears go away. Instead, I just become annoyed by spirits who like to frighten people and hang onto living people's energy. And I find the memories of the past that haunt buildings fascinating, almost like a history book lodged in the wall.

The last thing one wants to be in a house- or person-cleansing, an exorcism if you like, is fearful. Fear just puts us in the wrong frame of mind for the work we are there to do. Our sensitivity to spirit becomes inaccessible because we narrow our auric field instead of expanding it, and we activate the wrong part of the brain, producing the wrong chemicals in the body to be able to think clearly. Basically, we will want to flee and that's not helpful.

When I see 'an attachment' with someone, a thought-form or a spirit person who wants to hang around on the Earth, I become totally focussed on it, a bit like a wolf that has seen prey. I wait until I can remove it quietly and with minimum fuss, then send it into the light. This is not something for an inexperienced medium, healer or psychic to do and it is important to understand why the attachment is there to prevent it happening again. Without exception the person it has attached itself to has opened up to it, often through the use of non-prescription drugs, alcohol, the use of a ouija board, or by being in the company of someone who is doing something like that. Those who are naturally psychic will attract more because that is in their nature but their attitude is all-important. If they read horror books and watch that kind of film because it fascinates them, they will eventually have a problem.

Now, of course, I don't want anyone reading this to think that they might pick up a spare dead person with nastiness on their mind at the drop of a hat. No, that doesn't happen. But we all have tools that are there quite naturally to tell us when what we are doing is stupid from a spiritual safety point of view. Our insides will tell us that we don't like it even if we find it enervating and exciting; our gut will say, "Run away." Do so.

If you do become unstuck, then find a reputable medium through your local Spiritualist church. Don't go running around looking for just anyone to help; it's far better to go to someone who has a good reputation and not all mediums know how to deal with the scary stuff. A lot of mediums prefer to hang around with unicorns and fluffy spirits and won't even consider the presence of nasty spirit people as being possible. Wrong. On the whole, most spirit people are nice, like most Earthly people. However, there are rogues and just because someone's dead doesn't make them an angel.

Places where nasty things have happened also contain a nasty energy and these places attract nasty spirits. Of course, Nazi gas chambers are not going to feel nice, for example, and horrid spirit people tend to hang around together just as they do in this world. So if somewhere feels nasty, it probably is.

Fear can also present itself on this path in life for all sorts of other reasons. There is the fear of lack, fear of illness, fear of death... well, fear of pretty much anything is possible. Some people go to see mediums and psychics to ask for advice about their fears. They basically want someone else to tell them how to get round problems and how to live. They ask questions like, "Will I get some money to pay my bills?" or "Will I find someone to love?" The problem with this is that it is not a sensitive's job to make predictions for you, but people can be given suggestions by loved ones in spirit. These spirit people would have done the same thing when on the Earth and they continue to do that from the spirit side of life. But just because someone is in spirit, it doesn't mean that they know everything.

There are of course some enlightened spirits who do, but when it comes to Earthly and mundane things it's our life and we need to sort things out ourselves. That's the point – to live through difficulty and joy as an apparent individual, but with unconditional love and compassion to the fore. Generally, if someone in spiritual form has advice for their loved one on Earth, as long as the medium doesn't get in the way, it will come out. And if the answer one is seeking cannot be given because one needs to sort it for themselves, then that's all there is to it.

CHAPTER ELEVEN

ENVIRONMENT

I am writing this in December and it is 11 degrees Celsius out there! This makes no sense to me as I remember being snowed in regularly as a child over the Christmas break from school. I have lived in the countryside and villages for most of my life and the weather has a greater effect on life away from towns. Yes, towns do have slippery pavements and icy roads, but there is more traffic and things clear more rapidly. I used to expect to be stuck indoors during the winter at least once – but not now. I don't remember there being much flooding either when I was a kid. This was a rare thing. I'm sure some scientist has come up with statistics to say that everything is the same as ever; but, I'm sorry, I don't believe their figures especially when the weather presenters talk about 'unusually high winter temperatures'. Clearly, the inconvenient truth is upon us.

So what is the cause and what can we do about it? Well, various spirit guides tell us that as we are not separate as people, we are also not separate from nature. There are clues to this in all sorts of spiritual literature, including the words said by an orthodox vicar when we are buried: "Ashes to ashes, dust to dust." Science also tells us that we are made of stars, made of the same things that the Earth is made of, and that the laws of cause and effect apply to absolutely everything and everyone.

There is no-one and nothing excluded from that although, as We Are One, it is not necessarily personal in its outcome. Cause and effect, or karma, doesn't automatically affect us as individuals with like for like but it still gets us. Even if you are the world's best recycler and a gentle rainbow warrior, while some idiots are keeping all their lights on and driving gas-guzzling cars, you will be affected. Of course, we must start with ourselves and, as we have free will, we can't enforce our beliefs on others. But, frankly, perhaps we should or there won't be an Earth for our kids and grandkids to experience life on. Personally, I would like to see a greater influence on our habits enforced by well-informed governments. And that's the trouble, because no-one seems able to decide who is well-informed about the environment. It's an inconvenient truth, isn't it? People in power have tough choices to make about jobs and welfare now, as well as looking to the future, though surely it's a no-brainer: what's the point of protecting jobs and big corporations' money if there's not going to be a planet to live on in the future anyway?

My own inspirers tell me that the planet is going through 'a natural warming cycle' but that the habits of mankind have increased the temperature and the speed at which the warming happens. They tell me that it is still possible to make changes but that the way we live now is unsustainable and we have to find other ways of living. It appears that this alteration will happen within my lifetime. I am in my fifties now, so before I am a very old lady I shall have to learn to live differently. White Owl and Lana talked about the flooding, terrorist activity and financial crises long before they happened and with very specific information, so I don't see any reason to disbelieve their other predictions. They are very gentle in what they say as they don't like to engender fear, but suffice it to say that it is not spiritual to allow those who shouldn't have power to control our world. We must be more global in outlook and more determined in how we deal with bullies and power-hungry psychotics who are frightened of losing their money. Our kids also need to understand that they don't look better in clothing with labels on the outside that is made by exploited and underprivileged kids elsewhere. There must be a shift in emphasis away from materialism and towards good neighbourliness.

I expect, like me, that many of you have worried about the environment and probably felt quite small and insignificant. Have you asked yourself, "What can I do to make things better when I am only one person?" Yes, it's a tough one, but we can affect those around us by how we behave and you don't have to be Mother Teresa or Princess Diana (bless them both) to have an impact. I once bought a book on how to live more ethically and I have to say that it was quite an eye-opener; one can go from easy recycling through to belt-and-braces stuff, becoming vegan and growing one's own organic food. I've tried that and it's really hard, but I settled for doing my best.

I also believe that praying helps the planet and this is something we can all do. We should not think about the polluted world, the starving and the consumerist nature of society but instead, as with sending healing thoughts, try to remain detached and positive, praying for the beauty in the world, for those who have enough food to find a way of sharing it and for simplicity. These are positive thoughts and we are not adding to all the negativity with our own thoughts of sorrow. 'Fuel the good and starve the bad', is a way of thinking about it.

Here are the thoughts of a friend of mine in spirit, on the state of the environment. I call him Mr Elk and he is very much one of those displeased Native Americans.

"Ah, I am pleased to be able to speak about this. The Earth is very close to my heart as it should be to all people. It makes no sense to me that those who are on the Earth should treat it with such disdain. Is it the usual human way of ignoring significant things when they will actually have to do something about them? Is it laziness? Yes, in my opinion it is exactly that.

"People have very little concept of the life of the Earth. I am not talking about the life on it or within it or above it,

I am talking about the very core, the very heart of the Earth itself. Many people now call the Earth female, they speak of 'her' and call her female names. This is a good thing as she is just like a woman in that she carries life in her womb. Even if there is no baby in there, she has the potential to carry it; of course men have the ability to create life too, but one cannot do it without the other. It is a symbiosis.

"This is perhaps an easier way for people to think of the Earth as a symbiosis. Mankind lives on the Earth and needs her and the Earth in turn needs life upon, within and above her, for it is in her nature to nurture life. Without life, she dies. Her atmosphere would be ripped away without the trees and the jungle, and breathing humans and animals feed these.

"I wish mankind would get that. We, the indigenous peoples of the Earth, we get that. Most of those reading this will not get that because you no longer see yourselves as belonging to where you live. You probably don't feel the belonging unless you have lived somewhere for years and years. It gets even stronger when your ancestors have lived there too, for generations and generations.

"You have lost your connection to the planet, to your neighbourhood and to your people. I know the world is 'getting smaller', because you can all talk to each other through social media, telephones and suchlike, but that is not really talking as you cannot see each other's eyes. These are the windows to the soul and you are all hiding within your homes, machines and offices. It is really important to walk on the ground from time to time, barefoot, and to look at the sky without glass between you, even spectacles, and to touch a tree and an animal, to feel their hearts beating—then you know you are alive.

"You are told that exercise is good for you. Yes it is, but it is not so good when you do that indoors. Far better to be in nature and this can be found absolutely everywhere, even in the depths of the concrete jungle. A daisy here, a dandelion there, a park, a dog, the sky, the rain falling on you – all these things are available in towns, but far better in the countryside or by the sea, by a river or on a mountain with snow.

"Ah yes, all these things are far better in the wild. And it is important for the health of all that the wild still exists for your children and grandchildren. Please find a way of making that happen. I cannot help other than speak to you, as I am no longer in a body. I don't need the planet in the same way that you do; but know that it is unique and that the spirit can only learn about life in the unique way of Earth, on Earth and nowhere else. So it's down to you."

Be selfish and our world collapses. Be generous and our world evolves.

CHAPTER TWELVE

SPIRITUAL DEVELOPMENT

I hope that you have realised by now that the development of mediumship and kindred abilities does not make one a spiritual person. In fact, I don't think that Spiritualism specifies enough the dangers involved to the soul when it comes to the processes that we carry out in order to improve our ability to communicate with spirit people. It is taught in some organisations that those with mental health issues are at greater risk of bringing on a psychotic incident when training in psychic matters and this is quite true; but many people who have been told that they are mentally ill are in fact natural mediums and the medical profession doesn't understand that. The greatest danger I am talking about is the raising of the ego to a level of imbalance with the selfless self.

It is possible to become deluded, particularly when we seek the identity of our guides. It is exciting to find that a guide followed a spiritual path when last incarnate and that they have carried that on in the spirit world, but sometimes we can become hung up on who they were when last here. We can do that in two ways: we might think that we are extra special because we have a special person with us, or we can be so closed-minded to that possibility that we reject the guide and thereby lose something that could have been extremely useful in our lives.

It can also be a problem for people when they discover that they have inspirers who are not human! For exactly the same reasons as above, people struggle with the idea of animal, elemental or devic spirit guides, unless of course they understand the shamanic or pagan paths of spirituality. Some of us will hug a tree and feel the spirit within, but can't handle one talking to us. Alien guides? Although science now speaks openly of life on other worlds, even some psychics and mediums still ridicule this option. The easiest way to deal with our guides is to get to know them and if we are not happy then ask them to leave; but most people are guided by beings whom they don't know. As for angelic guides, it is apparently 'impossible' for this to happen – yet tens of thousands of people beg to differ. A few years ago I was demonstrating trance and, as far as the other mediums present were concerned, I was the best thing since sliced bread until... an angel spoke. All of a sudden, I was 'delusional' and everything that had impressed them previously became rubbish.

I have a guide who tells me about the future. It is a male voice and I have no idea who or what he is, but he is always right. He also tells me when someone is doing or saying something that could harm me and I am inspired with how to deal with that. Without exception, this inspiration has always worked; it has always been kind to the person who is being horrible even when they have needed to be spoken to in a tough way, perhaps publicly. Sometimes it has taken years for the application to complete but I no longer doubt the outcome because it always comes. In such situations, I am not looking to harm anyone in return but for that person to wake up, to smell the roses and stop applying manure to them. I have other guides whom I have known very well since childhood and others who have turned up later in life. Some come for a while and I have never been conscious of them again, but I know that they will be there if needed. I do have some guides who were famous when on the Earth. Some of these say exactly who they were and others use an alias, but all people have to do is to feel into a guide's energy and they will know exactly who they are.

I think that one of the most important faculties we need in our development is an open mind. If we close the mind then we are limiting our experience. I have seen, felt and heard things that I can't explain yet I know that they are real. This goes way beyond physical phenomena and talking with fairies, I'm talking about the very structure of the world not being what I thought it was. I have been in rooms that have bent, warped and stretched. I have seen transfiguration of living people upon the faces of mediums, and I have seen animals transfigure people and had animals transfigure me. I have been inside trees and become them. I have been to other worlds and other rooms that are just outside ours and yet are light years away. There is nothing that is not possible in life. When we open our minds to the endless journeys and possibilities of life, we find that mediumship and psychic abilities make more sense.

And if you are trying to develop spiritually, don't even think about working in an environment that is disharmonious. It is better to sit alone than in a group where there is aggravation – all you will do is pick up on it and then waste energy protecting yourself. Instead, look for people who genuinely want everyone in the group to grow and to learn as much as themselves. If you get a bad feeling about a venue or group, don't go back or don't go in the first place. It may not be that the leader or teacher is horrible; there could be someone else there who is a nasty piece of work. As a teacher, I have seen this situation a few times, when someone has behaved really badly in their material life, tried to separate this from their spiritual life and brought this deception to seminars, messing up lots of people around them.

If you are someone who has not learned how to see where the problem lies in a group and how to separate yourself from that, then you will be affected because you are sensitive. So how do you do that? Listen to the 'dodgy feelings' that you have, you know, the "Hmm, I can't quite put my finger on it, but something's wrong" feeling; then ask your guides, whether you know them or not, to protect you from this influence. Don't get stressed and believe that you're going to get eaten up by something evil – why would you be, you're a nice person aren't you? Instead, just send out a gentle thought of love and healing and then leave it alone. If your guide says, "Leg it!" then do so, but don't scare yourself. Be in a group that feels lovely and ask for the inspiration to know when things are not quite right; meditate every day and get to know your guides.

What makes a person more suitable to one particular area of development over another? People incarnate with innate abilities. Some have the ability to cook marvellous food and others are painters, for example; these abilities come from a variety of sources, one of course being genetics and another being the interests and behaviour of their parents. My children's father and I are not particularly interested in sport although we both love walking and nature. My sons never did well in sport at school although they love to be outdoors. The younger son was actually an extremely speedy runner but it doesn't interest him – if we had been interested in running then perhaps he would be an athlete now. We all influence those with whom we live. Again, both my sons are aware of spirit and interact with spirit people but are not interested in furthering this much. The reason for this is the same for both of them: they have seen the abuse that I have experienced within Spiritualism and have therefore lost interest, which is totally understandable.

Another influence on the spiritual work we do comes from past incarnations. I have been in holy orders more often than not, plus I have a nun for a doorkeeper, so I lean towards religious interests. I kind of can't help it, feeling more comfortable in an environment that is like being in cloisters. I also prefer silence and order yet confess that I do behave totally unlike our perception of how a nun should: I swear, have normal bodily functions, don't like washing in cold water and self-flagellation is not my thing either! I just love being in churches, temples and any other spiritual environment; note the word 'spiritual' here, since just as with apparently spiritual people, places are not always what they're supposed to be.

We all have a purpose for our incarnation that will also affect our development path. Some people incarnate because they want to make the world a better place. These souls have the ability to choose incarnation rather than just falling to Earth and gravitating to their next step in evolution without being aware of it. Their choices then involve parents, location and lifestyle that best suit their purpose. But don't think for one moment that most of these enlightened people remember all these things on incarnation; no, we all have states of awareness and we are all affected by the dampening field of Earthly life. There are people who obviously do know what they are about and we highlight them in society – people like the Dalai Lama and the Buddha. We must also not assume that these enlightened ones are only going to turn up in important or grand jobs: small ponds still need enlightened little fishes. But we can be reassured that these bright beings are not going to be the nasty people of the world, rather the ones who make us stand back and ask, "What or who is that?" because their light is massive and kind of confusing.

If you have come to the Earth with your mediumship button pressed, then there will be a specific way that is special for you that you can work in. Perhaps you have come into a home filled with music, then it would make sense that you would be interested in sound therapy. I came into a psychic household where there was a fascination with words and expression, thus I am a trance medium and spiritual writer. Sometimes the opposite happens, when someone is squeezed into suppression and the gift of spiritual expression bursts out later in life. Such suppression can even bring on mental illness because the medium is being forced to deny part of what they are, which is a dreadful thing. But other times, when the bursting comes it is instantaneous enlightenment. There are so many ways in which the spirit moves.

People learn in different ways. Some have to see something in order to understand or write it down, while others have to hear. This seems to be true of mediumship too. A very visual person is usually clairvoyant and someone who listens well is clairaudient. If one is particularly sensitive to feelings then clairsentience will be enhanced beyond the normal level that everyone has. Simple 'knowing' is slightly in a different area of awareness involving none of the usual senses and this tends to be there right from birth. These gifts are often suppressed but can be awoken as we develop the ability to notice them. That's the thing – noticing. It may be all there but we just don't pick up on it.

Of course, no two clairvoyants or empaths are the same and there are many ways in which to develop spiritually. We all use the same mechanisms but our interpretation and our library of experience will affect how we express our abilities. We must never try to be someone else, nor listen to a teacher who only wants us to work like they do.

CHAPTER THIRTEEN

THE FUTURE OF RELIGION

There is none.

Spirituality and religion do not go together. Religion creates disharmony. Spirituality is our natural state and is divine. Religion is man-made and is purely a system devised in order to try to classify the unclassifiable. There are insufficient words to express how it feels to be aware of God and certainly no dogma or creed that can keep us in that awareness.

IF YOU HAVE ENJOYED THIS BOOK...

Local Legend is committed to publishing the very best spiritual writing, both fiction and non-fiction. You might also enjoy:

THE QUIRKY MEDIUM

Alison Wynne-Ryder (ISBN 978-1-907203-47-3)

Alison is the co-host of the TV show *Rescue Mediums*, in which she puts herself in real danger to free homes of lost and often malicious spirits. Yet she is a most reluctant medium, afraid of ghosts! This is her amazing and often very funny autobiography, taking us 'back stage' of the television production as well as describing how she came to discover the psychic gifts that have brought her an international following.

Winner of the Silver Medal in the national Wishing Shelf Book Awards.

SIMPLY SPIRITUAL

Jacqui Rogers (ISBN 978-1-907203-75-6)

The 'spookies' started contacting Jacqui when she was a child and never gave up until, at last, she developed her psychic talents and became the successful international medium she is now. This is a powerful and moving account of her difficult life and her triumph over adversity, with many great stories of her spiritual readings. The book was a Finalist in The People's Book Prize national awards.

AURA CHILD

A I Kaymen (ISBN 978-1-907203-71-8)

One of the most astonishing books ever written, telling the true story of a genuine Indigo child. Genevieve grew up in a normal London family but from an early age realised that she had very special spiritual and psychic gifts. She saw the energy fields around living things, read people's thoughts and even found herself slipping through time, able to converse with the spirits of those who had lived in her neighbourhood. This is an uplifting and inspiring book for what it tells us about the nature of our minds and it was a Finalist in the Wishing Shelf Awards.

A UNIVERSAL GUIDE TO HAPPINESS

Joanne Gregory (ISBN 978-1-910027-06-6)

Joanne is an internationally acclaimed clairaudient medium with a celebrity contact list. Growing up, she ignored her evident psychic abilities, fearful of standing out from others; even later, despite witnessing miracles daily, her life was difficult. But then she began to learn the difference between the psychic and the spiritual and her life turned round.

This is her spiritual reference handbook – a guide to living happily and successfully in harmony with the energy that created our universe. It is the knowledge and wisdom distilled from a lifetime's experience of working with spirit.

A SINGLE PETAL

Oliver Eade (ISBN 978-1-907203-42-8)

Winner of the national Local Legend Spiritual Writing Competition, this page-turner is a novel of murder, politics and passion set in ancient China. Yet its themes of loyalty, commitment and deep personal love are every bit as relevant for us today as they were in past times. The author is an expert on Chinese culture and history, and his debut adult novel deserves to become a classic.

5P1R1T R3V3L4T10N5

Nigel Peace (ISBN 978-1-907203-14-5)

With descriptions of more than a hundred proven prophetic dreams and many more everyday synchronicities, the author shows us that, without doubt, we can know the future and that everyone can receive genuine spiritual guidance for our lives' challenges. World-renowned biologist Dr Rupert Sheldrake has endorsed this book as "...vivid and fascinating... pioneering research..." and it was national runner-up in The People's Book Prize awards.

RAINBOW CHILD

S L Coyne (ISBN 978-1-907203-92-3)

Beautifully written in language that is alternately lyrical and child-like, this is the story of young Rebekah and the people she discovers as her family settles in a new town far from their familiar home. As dark family secrets begin to unravel, her life takes many turns both delightful and terrifying as the story builds to a tragic and breathless climax that just keeps on going. This book, a Finalist in the national Wishing Shelf Awards, shows us how we look at others who are 'different'. Through the eyes of Rebekah, writing equally with passion and humour, we see the truth of human nature...

CELESTIAL AMBULANCE

Ann Matkins (ISBN 978-1-907203-45-9)

A brave and delightful comedy novel. Having died of cancer, Ben wakes up in the afterlife looking forward to a good rest, only to find that everyone is expected to get a job! He becomes the driver of an ambulance (with a mind of her own), rescuing the spirits of others who have died suddenly and delivering them safely home. This book is as thought-provoking as it is entertaining.

TAP ONCE FOR YES

Jacquie Parton (ISBN 978-1-907203-62-6)

This extraordinary book offers powerful evidence of human survival after death. When Jacquie's son Andrew suddenly committed suicide, she was devastated. But she was determined to find out whether his spirit lived on, and began to receive incredible yet undeniable messages from him… Several others also then described deliberate attempts at spirit contact. This is a story of astonishing love and courage, as Jacquie fought her own grief and others' doubts in order to prove to the world that her son still lives.

These titles are all available as paperbacks and eBooks.
Further details and extracts of these and many
other beautiful books may be seen at

www.local-legend.co.uk

Lightning Source UK Ltd.
Milton Keynes UK
UKOW06f1240280715

255966UK00009B/140/P